MINNESOTA

Natural Wonders of
MINNESOTA

SECOND EDITION

Exploring Wild and Scenic Places

MARTIN HINTZ

COUNTRY ROADS PRESS
NTC/Contemporary Publishing Group

Library of Congress Cataloging-in-Publication Data

Hintz, Martin.
    Natural wonders of Minnesota : exploring wild and scenic places / Martin
Hintz. — 2nd ed.
       p. cm. — (Natural wonders)
      Includes index.
      ISBN 0-658-00241-4
      1. Minnesota—Guidebooks.   2. Parks—Minnesota—Guidebooks.
3. Wildlife refuges—Minnesota—Guidebooks.   4. National parks and
reserves—Minnesota—Guidebooks.   5. Natural areas—Minnesota—
Guidebooks.   6. Natural history—Minnesota—Guidebooks.
7. Recreation areas—Minnesota—Guidebooks.   I. Title. II. Series.
F604.3.H565   2000
917.7604'5321—dc21   99-43630

Cover and interior design by Nick Panos
Cover photograph: Mississippi River. Copyright © Zane Williams/Panoramic Images
Interior illustrations and map copyright © Gigi Bayliss. Spot illustrations copyright
© Barbara Kelly
Picture research by Jill Birschbach

Published by Country Roads Press
A division of NTC/Contemporary Publishing Group, Inc.
4255 West Touhy Avenue, Lincolnwood (Chicago), Illinois 60712-1975 U.S.A.
Copyright © 2000, 1996 by Martin Hintz
Printed in the United States of America
International Standard Book Number: 0-658-00241-4

00 01 02 03 04 05 ML 19 18 17 16 15 14 13 12 11 10 9 8 7 6 5 4 3 2 1

To my sister, Gretchen Wronka, and her husband Gunther,
as well as nephews Peter, Hans, and Joe—
all are true Minnesotans who appreciate
the natural wonders of their state.

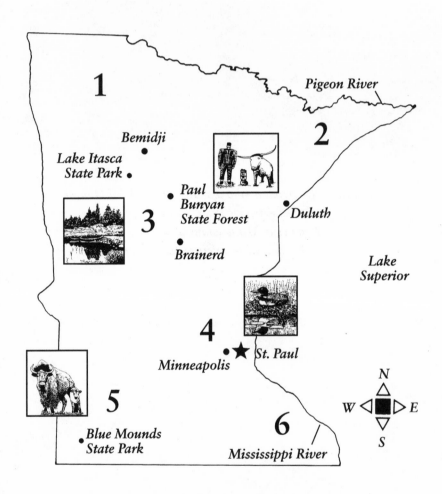

1

Pigeon River

2

Bemidji

Lake Itasca
State Park

Paul
Bunyan
State Forest

3

Brainerd

Duluth

Lake
Superior

4

Minneapolis ★ St. Paul

5

6

N

W ◁ ▣ ▷ E

S

Blue Mounds
State Park

Mississippi River

Minnesota
(Figures correspond with chapter numbers.)

Contents

Acknowledgments   XI
Introduction   XIII

1 Northwest 1

Buffalo River State Park 5
Chippewa National Forest 6
Lake Bronson State Park 8
Lake Itasca State Park 11
White Earth State Forest 15
Tamarac National Wildlife Refuge 19
Zippel Bay State Park 20

2 Northeast 25

Boundary Waters Canoe Area Wilderness 30
Cascade River State Park 32
Gunflint Trail 35
Lutsen–Tofte Area 37
Superior Hiking Trail 43
Superior National Forest 46
Tettegouche State Park 49

3 Central 53

Charles A. Lindbergh State Park 55
Crow Wing State Park 58
Father Hennepin State Park 61
Foothills State Forest/Spider Lake Ski Trail 63

Mille Lacs Kathio State Park and Rum River
   State Forest 66
Moose Lake Recreational Area 70
Otter Tail County 71
Paul Bunyan State Forest 74
St. John's University 78

4 Metro Area 81

Hennepin Parks 82
Ramsey County 93
Minnesota Valley National Wildlife Refuge 102
Fort Snelling State Park 108

5 Southwest 113

Blue Mounds State Park 117
Camden State Park 121
Glacial Lakes State Park 123
Lac qui Parle State Park 125
Lake Shetek State Park 128
Pipestone National Monument/Split Rock Creek
   Recreation Area 130

6 Southeast 135

Bear Lake Wetlands 138
Beaver Creek Valley State Park 138
Forestville/Mystery Cave State Park 141
Hay Creek Management Area, Richard J. Dorer
   Memorial State Forest 146
Lake Louise State Park 147
Lamprey Pass Wildlife Management Area 151
Nerstrand–Big Woods State Park 151

Great River Bluffs State Park (formerly O.L. Kipp
    State Park) 154
Rice Lake State Park 157
Reno Bottoms Delta/Reno Management Unit,
    Richard J. Dorer Memorial State Forest 160
Whitewater State Park 162
Whitewater Wildlife Management Area 165

Appendix 167
Index 171

Acknowledgments

Thanks are offered to the dozens of Minnesotans I have met on my many travels around their wonderful state. There were innumerable fishing guides, naturalists, county workers, interpreters, resort owners, museum personnel, local tourism representatives, hikers, pie bakers, people on the street, rock climbers, cyclists, tribal leaders, butterfly counters, and folks who could talk with wolves. Their friendliness, concern, and interest in this project were greatly appreciated. A special nod goes to Tom Crain of Media Inroads; Dave Bergman and Linda Robertson of the Minnesota Division of Tourism; to all the gang at the Minnesota Department of Natural Resources and its division of parks, especially to Kate Brady, Sheila Gebhard, and Dan Collins; to the many other state, county, and federal employees whose love of the land and its creatures was so obvious; and to outdoor writers Thomas F. Waters and Craig Charles.

Introduction

The breeze rustles the maples thickly carpeting the upper ridge line behind the interpretive buildings of the Forest Resource Center in Lanesboro. I had just returned from watching center staffers clamber like monkeys through the Group Challenges Course, a series of rope climbs and swinging bridges that teaches teams to work together. The private, nonprofit corporation promotes the responsible use, renewal, and appreciation of natural resources from its base in southeastern Minnesota's bluff country. The course helps a group learn to cooperate, solve problems, communicate, trust, and—yes—survive.

The conclusion was One Small Step, a 180-foot-long zipline exit that brings a rush to the heart. You sweep downhill through the trees with everything a blur until you reach the bottom. It takes a minute before your heart catches up. What follows is the requisite rest and recuperation time, with all the accompanying "great job, good work" backslapping.

The center's training regime is a metaphor for learning about and preserving the natural wonders of this Land of 10,000 Lakes. There is the initial challenge: the hard, ongoing team effort in making sure the forests, wetlands, prairies, and wildlife are protected. It is a tough, rugged job. Not a little bit scary. But then everything comes together. We all make it through and learn from the experience.

This book offers merely the tiniest peek at all of Minnesota's natural wonders. Prairies, sloughs, cliffs, woodlots, lakes, rivers, oak-dotted savannas, national forests, county parks, nature centers, urban hideaways. There is so much to see and enjoy. There are dedicated, concerned people who can point you in the right direction, whether a park ranger; the owner of a bed-and-breakfast; a canoe outfitter; a bike-shop owner; or the local butcher, baker, and candlestick maker. "Gopher Landers" love to show off and brag about their state. Rightly so.

However, looking at how Minnesota's natural environment has been changed over the past generations is sobering: resources depleted, wetlands drained, forests downed, animals killed. Ensuring that we retain remnants of these natural wonders for the next generation is our responsibility today. And there are positives: Reforestation, fish stocking, and land acquisition for parks are only a few of the chalk marks on the upbeat side. When traveling Minnesota and experiencing its recreational opportunities, look around, observe, admire, and support actions that ensure clean water and fresh air.

There is plenty of help on this road to discovery, whether for hiking, cycling, fishing, hunting, backpacking, snowshoeing, canoeing, houseboating, skiing, snowmobiling, or whatever else your outdoors spirit desires. References with addresses and phone numbers are included with each listing in the book. But you can start with the following contacts for your preliminary planning. Augment these contacts with local tourism information centers, forest ranger offices, and parks personnel. You won't go wrong. And remember these are simply a few of my favorite places, with additional recommendations from trusted friends and suggestions from natural resource personnel.

Find your own Nature's Hit Parade. It might be under the soughing red pines in Hayes Lake State Park. Or on the wave-washed shore of Kabetogama Lake in the Voyageurs National Park. Or somewhere along the Cut Foot Sioux or the Suomi Hills hiking trails. It might be a sensory experience, such as hearing a sunset loon cry or seeing a quivering newborn fawn step from the mist.

Tune in to the world. Listen and watch. There is so much to Minnesota. On the wild side.

Quick State Facts

Total area: 84,068 square miles, of which 4,059 square miles are water (more than any other state)

Miles long: 406

Miles wide: 348

Capital: St. Paul

State gemstone: Lake Superior agate

State bird: common loon

State fish: walleye

State flower: showy lady's slipper

State grain: wild rice

State mushroom: yellow morel

State tree: red pine

State song: "Hail, Minnesota!"

Number of counties: 87

Nicknames: Land of 10,000 Lakes, Gopher State, North Star State (translated from its motto, L'Etoile du Nord)

Altitude ranges: from 602 feet above sea level at Lake Superior to 2,230 feet in the Misquah Hills north of the lake

Drainage: Minnesota waters flow north to the Hudson Bay, east to the Atlantic Ocean, and south to the Gulf of Mexico; 57 percent of the state is drained by the Mississippi River.

1

Northwest

A mix of prairie, lake, and forest, northwestern Minnesota snuggles up to its Canadian border on the north and North Dakota on the west. A chain of state forests, along with the Chippewa National Forest, dapple the map in splashes of verdant coloring. Each forest and open-space unit has its distinctive personality, history, and resources. All have been affected by humans for thousands of years, starting from the wandering hunters skirting the edges of glaciers to this week's carload of swimsuited tourists. Archaeologists have discovered pottery shards, bones, arrowheads, spear points, and other refuse tossed aside a hundred generations ago. We should all be grateful that today's Adopt a Highway program, whereby community groups and businesses volunteer to police highway ditches and roadsides, already cleans up contemporary refuse. In more recent centuries, various Native American nations also called northwestern Minnesota their home, well before whites moved into the neighborhood. Then came the settlers, first as loggers and then as farmers.

Glacial Lake Agassiz, which withdrew from northwestern Minnesota 10,000 years ago, had flattened the land. Only the erosion-exposed sandstone ledges and valleys cut by long-ago rivers provide much variety in the sandy, rock-bottomed landscape. In many places drainage was poor after the vast prehistoric lake retreated. However, hydrogeologists say that the water table remained high, which created bogs and marshes throughout much of this area of the state. This created great habitat for moose, with all the accompanying critters in the food chain, from bugs to bobcat, lynx, wolf, skunk, deer, beaver, loons, herons, grebes, and hundreds of other species.

Homesteaders tried to shape the land to their uses. Some were successful and others were not. Farsighted planners and look-ahead environmentalists then stepped in to rehabilitate damaged land. Witness the turn of events in one small neighborhood. As the 1900s opened, Alva Hendershot moved into a logged-over area about 20 miles southeast of Roseau. The Hendershots farmed there for a number of years before pulling up stakes and moving on in the search for deeper soil more suitable for corn and wheat. The Hayes clan also settled nearby and hung on longer. As more and more farmers left the area, the idea for a state park in the vicinity was suggested in 1958, but it wasn't until 1967 that the legislature gave the go-ahead for a park development. A need was perceived for waterbased recreational opportunities, but nothing much was done until the early 1970s, when a dam was constructed along the North Branch of the Roseau River at the suggestion of landowner A. F. Hayes. Remains of the Hayes's original farm buildings, as well as graves of deceased family members, can be seen along a trail that goes through what is now Hayes Lake State Park. Kids who splash in Hayes Lake probably have no idea that this was once only part of the peaceful Roseau River. Also those long-dead pioneers who are buried there are quietly blissful of the changes in landscape and land-use philosophy as well. The town of Roseau is home to Polaris Industries, where snowmobiles and other recreation vehicles are made.

There are numerous other natural attractions and sites (sights) throughout northwestern Minnesota that draw woodswise outdoor lovers. The snakelike Red Lake River meanders along a convoluted 195 miles of great canoeing, with easy riffles and camping along the way. State Highway 11 between Baudette and Greenbush is a state-designated Wildflower Route. The "Wilderness Drive" from Baudette to Warroad through the Beltrami Island State Forest unrolls miles of Kodak-perfect scenery.

There's the Voyageur's Path along the Rainy River; the Can-Am recreation trail that connects the far northwest hunk of the state with Canada; the Paul Bunyan Recreational Trail from Bemidji to Brainerd, with innumerable connections to other trail units; and 400 miles of groomed snowmobile trails around Thief River Falls, home base for Arctic Cat.

The Bluewater/Wabana area is part of a chain of lakes in the center of Itasca County, 15 miles north of Grand Rapids. Fisher folk know that largemouth and rock bass lurk in the depths of the 2,215-acre Wabana Lake and that yellow perch and lake trout are popular catches in Bluewater. The latter, with 364 acres, has a depth of 102 feet—more than enough space for lunkers of all types. The Trout Lake Recreation Area is also part of that lake system, much of which lies within the Chippewa National Forest. Trout Lake is a 4,500-acre parcel that includes a historic farmsite, camping, and a canoe access. You'll be assured of peace and quiet because the entire semiprimitive district is off-limits to motorized vehicles, except for cars on their way to the campgrounds. Stand at the portage at Bee Cee Lake after a long, slow canoe paddle from the east at Moonshine Lake. You'll catch the cry of loons, the shrill chatter of jays, and the splash of herons in the marsh. It's only a short canoe carry, barely a quarter mile, to put in again at Trout Lake for more exploring. You can access Trout Lake at the intersection of State

Highways 49 and 50 on the east, County Highway 335 on the south, and County Highway 326 on the north. Once you park your car, don't even think about ignitions for however long you can enjoy your getaway.

From an eagle's skyborne vantage point, the splash of lakes in Itasca County is a dazzling display of jewel drops. It was as if Paul Bunyan had opened his money purse and all the silver coins fell from the clouds to dapple the land: Murphy, Birch, Potato, Plantation, Sand, Cutaway, Little Wabana, Picker, Bosely, Dead Horse, Johnson, Inky, Tadpole—the list of lakes is almost endless. Early mapmakers came close to running out of names.

Indian Creek State Forest Road off State Highway 44 cuts into the heart of Two Inlets State Forest, past Becker County's Duck Lake, and on to Two Inlets Lake. You connect with Two Inlets State Forest Road to get to the boat-launch site on the western shore of Two Inlets Lake. Spending still summer afternoons on that shimmering surface is unrivaled for peace of mind. An occasional bass helped into the boat via a rod and reel doubles the day's pleasure. For those with a more active frame of mind in the winter, the 28 miles of snowmobile trails through the forest in the vicinity of Two Inlets Lake make for a rambling trek through the pines and aspen, connecting with trails in Hubbard County.

The counties in northwestern Minnesota—whether Kittson, Norman, Red Lake, Beltrami, or any of the others—have just as much to offer: a breeze through the hair, a bit of sunburn, and maybe a tolerable mosquito or two, as well as plenty of whitetail sightings, walleye in the frying pan, trailside rocks on which to sit, cool ripples along backcountry streams, deep powdery snow for schussing and snowshoeing, resorts and lodges, and mile after mile of nobody. Come for a day or a week and experience it all firsthand.

Buffalo River State Park

The Red River valley was once a sea of prairie grasses extending from horizon to horizon, broken only by the meandering Buffalo River and clumps of bank-hugging trees. Rehabilitated from that expanse, after the farmers' plows did their job generations in the past, is the state park and the Bluestem Prairie Scientific and Natural Area, owned by The Nature Conservancy.

For any flower lovers, Buffalo River in northwestern Minnesota certainly is the place to be. Some 250 prairie grasses and flowers grow there in a profusion of yellow, blue, red, and white blooms amid the towering green stalks. The river bisects the park, with cottonwoods flinging their fluffy whiteness into May's spring breezes. Basswood, oak, elm, and ash fill in the gaps along the banks.

Ten thousand years ago, the vast Lake Agassiz covered the valley. Named after famed geologist Louis Agassiz, the "father of glacial geology," the glacial lake shaped the landscape by depositing thick, rich silt as it drained away when half-mile-thick glaciers melted. The rolling lake bottom was broken by gravel ridges, called "beach lines." Settlers who came in the mid-19th century were awestruck by the black soil, which seemed to grow anything planted.

Where: Buffalo River State Park is located 4½ miles east of Glyndon and 30 miles west of Detroit Lakes or 13 miles east of Moorhead. Entrance to the park is via U.S. Route 10.

Other: In the summer a park naturalist and interpreters from local college botany and environmental programs lead hikers on expeditions around the park. Check at the park office for times and topics of these jaunts. Information boards around the campground and picnic area also list subjects that cover the park geology, wildlife, plants, and history.

For more information: Buffalo River State Park Manager, Box 256, Route 2, Glyndon, MN 56547. Call 218-498-2124.
Pets: Leashed or leave 'em at the kennel.
Best time to visit: Year-round.
Activities: Camping, hiking, bird-watching, swimming, and skiing.

Chippewa National Forest

You know you have arrived in the North Woods when you pull up to the parking lot near the Chippewa National Forest headquarters building at Cass Lake. The log building, built in 1935, is made of native red pine and was constructed by hardy Finnish craftsmen with the help of the Civilian Conservation Corps and the Works Progress Administration. The massive structure encompasses 8,500 square feet, with more than 16,000 linear feet of logs that are from 10 to 16 inches in diameter. A 50-foot-high chimney for the lobby fireplace is made from glacial boulders (yes, boulders, not pebbles) that were found in the area. At least 265 tons of rock were used in building that rustic heating unit. Don't worry about the gnarled appearance of the building's railings along the stair-wells—they were hand-fitted from selected maple and pine trees that were twisted and damaged by frost, the unique shapes just the way nature intended them to be. True to the Forest Service's mission of preservation, trees that were on the site were moved and replanted before construction of the headquarters began. In 1976 the structure was placed on the National Register of Historic Places.

Leaving by the front door, the visitor faces 660,000 acres of federally managed prime timber, streams, bald eagles, bears, campgrounds, hiking trails, bass, trailing arbutis, butterflies, wild strawberries, and owls. The forest boundary encompasses about 1.6 million acres with a melange of state, county, and private ownership, in addition to the aforementioned Forest Service presence.

The first native people who lived here—the Anishinabe (Original Man), the Dakota, Windigo, and Cree—moved calmly through the white oak and pine and made little impact on the environment. European settlement, as happened throughout most of Minnesota, changed the land dramatically with its logging, farming, dams, and road building. Today the Forest Service has to reconcile the traditional and the contemporary in protecting the diverse ecosystem. The service now allows a certain amount of timber harvesting in a manner that ensures there will be such a forest to use far into the future.

The national forest was established in 1908 after years of political arguing. But the deals eventually were made, the compromises reached, the boundaries set, and the forest born. Among the leaders of the movement to create the Chippewa National Forest was the Minnesota Federation of Women's Clubs. The group lobbied hard to protect stands of timber from loggers and demanded just compensation for the Native American population who lived there.

Is hiking available? Try the more than 160 miles of trails. Want to try canoeing? There are 900 miles of rivers and 1,321 lakes. Where to stay? How about 26 developed campgrounds from which to choose. Fishing? There are fishing piers at Gilstad Lake, Cut Foot Sioux, Knutson Dam, and Cass Lake. Birds? Look for bald eagles. The forest has about 1,400 acres perfect for eagle habitats, providing one of the largest concentrations of the birds in North America. One hundred eighty-six pairs of eagles have been located there since the mid-1990s. Most were successful in raising at least one young, and some were even responsible for triplets. Look for their nests in tall pines, usually near a lakeshore where they can fish. The nests are hard to miss. These lofty wonders measure up to 10 feet across and can weigh more than 4,000 pounds of twigs, leaves, and brush. The best time to watch the eagles is from mid-March to the end of November.

Where: The forest sprawls across Itasca and Cass Counties, with several major access points. U.S. Route 2 cuts through the center of the Chippewa with the Forest Service headquarters building on the highway, along the west side of Cass Lake. Secure a map from the Forest Service office there for other entry points. Major highways running through the forest include State Highways 6 and 46. County Highways include 48, 45, 4, 37, 8, 39, and others, plus dozens of forest roads accessible to visitors.

For more information: Chippewa National Forest, Forest Supervisor, Route 3, Box 244, Cass Lake, MN 56633. Call 218-335-8600; or you can contact any of the district rangers at Blackduck, Cass Lake, Deer River, and Walker. For campground reservations, call Parknet, 877-444-6770. Website: www.reserveusa.com.

Pets: Keep them at home or leashed.

Best time to visit: All year.

Activities: Hiking, camping, fishing, bird-watching, snowmobiling, hunting.

Lake Bronson State Park

You can't get much more northwest in Minnesota than at Lake Bronson. The park takes up the far corner of Kittson County, one mile east of the city of Lake Bronson. The park is in a delicate transition zone between the flat Red River valley and rolling hills blanketed with aspen. Subsequently, a visitor can see how the prairie merges with the forestland, supporting a wide variety of wildlife. Bird-watchers can observe grouse, sandpipers, and dozens of other species. Those who go in for bigger game might even have the opportunity to watch moose wallowing in the back bog lands and black bear rummaging through the berry bushes.

On human terms Lake Bronson is also a transition between wildlife and recreational developments, such as a great swimming beach and canoe-launch sites. Of course in the winter, snowmobilers and skiers can get out into the woods for extra action. An observation tower near the trailer sanitation area provides a fine overview of the park.

Lake Bronson

Today's Lake Bronson was formed by the damming of the South Branch of the Two River. Contemporary engineers might have taken their construction clue from prehistory in creating this modern recreational area. A mere 8,000 years ago, a dimple in time when it comes to geological eons, glacial Lake Agassiz covered the pancake-shaped region from Canada through North Dakota. At the time piles of ice blocked the runoff in the far north to create that ancient lake. When the mountains of ice cubes finally melted, the lake receded and left gravel piles in broad, sweeping ridges. Some of these wavy ancient shorelines are seen in the park. Visitors can tell their locations, especially in streambeds where the ridges create small rapids as they tumble downstream. Today's lake was created when a drought in the 1930s dried up the wells around the towns of Lake Bronson and Hallock. The state decided it would help to dam the river and ensure a ready supply of water for the future.

But there were problems. Ma Nature had some tricks up her voluminous sleeves.

When dam construction started in 1936, it was discovered that the site contained quicksand that was more than 100 feet deep. Engineer Cliff Holland then thought up a system whereby the weight of the dam forced water up through six-inch pipes, thereby solidifying the soil base. Woods walkers near the dam can still see the pipes in the spillway wall.

Take a copy of the mammal checklist secured at the visitors center when you wander through Lake Bronson State Park. The handy roll call of critters is a fun way to observe all the life around you. For the record more than 200 species of birds have been counted in the park, as well as 53 types of mammals and 24 types of reptiles and amphibians.

Where: You can get to the park via County State Aid Highway 28.

For more information: Lake Bronson State Park Manager, Box 9, Lake Bronson, MN 56734. Call 218-754-2200.

Hours: The park is open year-round, with the gates opening at 8:00 A.M. and closing at 10:00 P.M. However registered campers can come and go at any time of day or night

Amenities: The park has 194 semimodern campsites (35 of the sites have electricity). There is also a trailer dump station and flush toilets and showers for woodsy luxury. A primitive group camp can accommodate 50 folks and includes a covered picnic shelter. Speaking of outdoor dining, a regular picnic area holds 110 tables, so there is usually a place to put out tart, homemade coleslaw and pickled pigs' feet from your basket. There is also a snack bar if anyone desires ice cream for dessert. Total up 14 miles of hiking trails, 10 miles of snowmobile trails, six miles of cross-country trails, five miles of bike trails, and you have a park complex accommodating most outdoor interests. Best of all the park is so far to the northwest that you will never feel crowded. Leave the in-line skates at home.

Pets: Tied and leashed.
Best time to visit: All year.
Activities: Hiking, camping, bird-watching, picnicking, biking.
Other: Don't pick up dead wood for fires. You can get firewood from the park staff at the visitors center. However, portable stoves and grills are permitted.

Lake Itasca State Park

Okay, okay. Take it easy now. The cool water rushes over the moss-coated rocks at the headwaters of the Mississippi River

Headwaters of the Mississippi at Lake Itasca State Park

in Itasca State Park. "If you make it across without falling in, you'll have good luck and a long life," asserts Elizabeth Murray, a park naturalist. So what if the stream is barely 10 feet wide—it seems like stretching across a raging torrent when toddling across the rocks barefoot. But with a few acrobatic maneuvers to keep the balance, worthy of a high-wire artist in Walker Brothers Circus, I made it safely across—and back again—with a definite smugness.

The birthing area of the Mighty Miss can be found at the end of a 600-foot walkway from the parking lot, past park offices and gift shop, and under a towering pine umbrella to the lakeside. From this inconspicuous spot, the nation's largest river begins.

It's a wonder that anyone knows the name of the park, after all the convolutions it took to arrive at "Itasca." Adventurer Henry Rowe Schoolcraft originally suggested the name, which puts to bunk the legend that the lake was named after a lovely, love-stricken Indian maiden. In 1832 when Schoolcraft was led to the lake by Ozawindib, an Ojibway guide, he and a friend created the lake's name by combining the Latin words for "truth" and "head" by linking adjoining syllables. Subsequently you have *verITAS CAput*, meaning "true head." But before Schoolcraft put his mind to such word games, French trappers and traders knew the lake as Lac La Biche or Elk Lake. The voyageurs apparently thought the lake was shaped like the head of an elk. Yet the first recorded name for the park, given to it by the Ojibway, was Omushkos, which means "elk." The name had been used by the local Native Americans since the 1700s when the Ojibway Nation moved into the area.

Regardless of how and when it received an official name, Lake Itasca has been a state park since April 10, 1891. Of course, people had lived in the region for 8,000 years previously. You can see 900-year-old burial mounds and an ancient bison kill site (along Wilderness Drive near Elk Lake) where the large animals were driven over a cliff. Once crumpled at the bottom, they were easily skinned and carved up for food.

Jacob V. Brower, a Civil War veteran, local political hero, and amateur archaeologist, surveyed the land that is now the park on behalf of the Minnesota Historical Society. His mission was to find the real source of the Mississippi River. As he roamed the forest, he realized that once the lumber interests got hold of the property, it would be decimated. He then lobbied the state legislature and won enough concessions from that august body to have it agree to establish the park. Brower was named the park's first superintendent, followed by John Gibbs, whose daughter Mary succeeded him. Mary Gibbs was the first woman park commissioner in North America and continued her predecessors' fight to contain the ax-wielding timber companies, even when threatened with murder. She called the bluff of the good ol' boys and beat them at their own game. Backed by gun-toting sheriff's deputies, Gibbs even blasted open an illegal dam that a timber firm had built to raise the level of Lake Itasca so it could float nine million board feet downstream to the mills. If she had not courageously stepped in, the dam would have destroyed hundreds of acres of other pine stands. Thank heavens she had guts, brains, and fortitude in pursuit of her job. Otherwise the state's largest white pine tree might also have gone the way of many companions snatched away by the timber magnates. The tree, a 250-foot giant, still stands along Two Spot Trail.

The park has many interpretive programs designed for kids, oldsters, and everyone in between. Led by park naturalists, topics include learning the significance of the forest ecosystem and understanding how deer cope with their human neighbors. There are also campfire programs, afternoon activities for kids, hikes, and a special guest series. The latter consists of a funfilled evening of music, woods lore, and other entertainment, usually starting at 8:00 P.M. in the amphitheater located in the picnic area.

I suggest you climb to the top of the 100-foot-high Aiton Heights Fire Tower, with its parking lot indicated on maps along Wilderness Drive. From that lot it is only a half-mile walk over moderately hilly terrain to the tower's skinny legs. If you want to stroll longer, leave from the Douglas Lodge area. Signs at the observation deck high above the trees explain what is spread out before you over the Lake Itasca watershed.

Where: Itasca State Park is ringed by Clearwater County Highway 38, with the main entrance at the junction of County Highways 38 and 1 near the Forest Inn. Only 21 miles north of Park Rapids on U.S. Route 71, the park is one of the most popular in the state.

For more information: Itasca State Park Manager, Box 4, Lake Itasca, MN 56460-9701. Call 218-266-2114.

Pets: Leashed.

Best time to visit: Year-round.

Activities: Sightseeing, camping, hiking, cross-country skiing, stepping across the Mississippi River.

Other: Secure a copy of the park's *Wilderness Drive Auto Tour Guide* booklet ($1.00), which introduces motorists to the variety of plant and animal life found in the park. It also discusses the human and natural histories of the region. A cassette-tape tour is also available, telling of the park's geology, history, flora, and fauna. Both can be purchased for a modest amount at the Forest Inn, park headquarters, or the Douglas Lodge gift shops. *The Itasca Guidebook*, compiled and updated annually by park staff, is also available for $8.95. It has plenty of maps, articles on animals found in the park, trail guides, and other references.

Don't worry if you have forgotten your canoe, a trolling motor, fishing license, bait, depth finder, motorboat, or air compressor. Itasca Sports Rental (218-266-2150) can outfit the most unprepared camper, hiker, fisherman, or water buff. The shop has more than 160 bikes for rent, with helmets provided free. The staff can also provide bug spray, ice-cream bars, beach accessories, and other necessities for today's urban explorers testing the wilderness.

White Earth State Forest

It's a dim autumn dawn, with the sun just yawning over the horizon. Yet the Ojibway rice harvesters are ready for launching their canoes, eager to hit the marshes before the day's heat becomes too oppressive. Denny St. Clair, Dorothy and Darwin Stevens, and their friends are clustered at the weedy landing in a secret place deep in the heart of the White Earth Indian Reservation. The reservation enfolds and protects the White Earth State Forest as would a shawl over the shoulders of a tribal elder. The ricing season brings hours of backbreaking work, yet a good harvest can keep an Ojibway family in food and rent for another half a year. Prices vary from year to year for a pound of rice at the drying sheds; however, the wild rice has remained a bedrock economic staple in northwestern Minnesota since the dawn of human time . . . even if we don't discuss value from a dollar viewpoint.

St. Clair, who tired of city life after two decades of Twin Cities' concrete and bus exhaust, came back to the reservation to live amid the sweetly scented pines and whispering aspen. The forest was a place where his heart belonged, he intimated, the words coming carefully in the presence of an outsider. St. Clair crumbles a cigarette and spreads the minute flakes over the lake's backwater before beginning his day's labor. The sacred tobacco is a gift to the Spirit that keeps his family strong and healthy. "I suppose I am still a traditionalist. This ritual is important to me," he offers, sliding his canoe gracefully through the shallow water. The rice stalks tower over him, as he sits in the rear of the skinny, low-hung boat. His paddle stabs deeply into the muddy water as his brown-black eyes scout for a healthy stand of rice. Around him are the other harvesters, each respectful of the others' territory. There are usually two persons to a canoe: one standing to push with a long pole through the marsh and another using hand-carved wooden sticks called "knockers" to sweep the rice into the canoe bottom. The heavy heads of the ripe rice bend in front of them, the greener rice stays straight. Within a few days that too will be ready for harvest, which means a return visit.

St. Clair is used to both maneuvering and harvesting on his own. Yet with a partner or alone, the result is the same: protein-rich rice piles up as the day goes along. The heat rises, the mosquitoes are more fierce, arms tire, rice worms wiggle through the cache, dust causes sneezing—but the breeze clears the mind and the cry of a blue jay echoes across the lake. From the muffled distance come the drumbeats of other harvesters, knock-knock-knocking the rice into their boats. It is a trade-off: the work balanced by the freedom.

The Mah Konce drying barn, at the corner of State Highway 200 and County Highway 4 near Lake Goodwin, is the destination for many of the reservation's ricers. Presided over by Ani Kikiiwanaquat (whose Anglo name is Bob Shimek), the Mah Konce hand-operated roaster dries 350 pounds of rice at a time in a huge drum that rotates over a roaring blaze. A skilled drier must ensure even turns, to prevent scorching and the subsequent lower market value, to say nothing of angry harvesters who think of all the time and energy put into getting the rice to market. After the process is completed, the rice is sifted and bagged for sale. Visitors to the White Earth State Forest area know they can buy excellent rice at such outlets as Mantok Wild Rice at the corner of County Highway 26 and U.S. Route 59. And when there, don't forget to buy a jar of homemade gooseberry jam or a birch-bark "good luck" birdhouse as well.

Only Native Americans and Minnesota residents with a valid permit (hard to get, by the way) can harvest wild rice in the time-honored way. So if you come across a stand while canoeing Upper Rice Lake, Roy Lake, or North and South Twin Lakes, keep your hands to yourself. Rangers frown on hidden stashes of rice.

The glaciated nature of the White Earth State Forest has been its biggest protector. The ragged terrain, deep pothole lakes, and rocky soil kept the farmers away and safe from the agricultural development that changed the face of much of Minnesota. As such the forest's 160,502 acres are alive with red and white pine, spruce, elm, aspen, maple, and basswood. There are some brushy sections, interspersed with marshland and wild rice swamps. Lumbering is allowed within the forest, with about 475 acres harvested annually primarily for use in Bemidji's wafer-board plants. The state replants almost 200 acres of conifers a year, while logged aspen areas are left alone to regenerate themselves. You will notice clearings in the forest, which have been protected to provide shelters for deer.

There are plenty of recreational opportunities within White Earth State Forest. Arrow Point Campground is 18 miles west of the junction of U.S. Route 71 and State Highway 113. Turn north and drive 4½ miles on the Height of Land State Forest Road. This is a campground for the rugged set. You have to backpack your gear a quarter mile into the woods from the main parking lot. Reservations are recommended because the popular site has room only for eight, but there is a great swimming beach and unrivaled fishing on Big Rock Lake.

Winter sports enthusiasts can snowmobile along the 65 miles of Forest Service roads that link the various ranger stations, boat launches, and canoe-access points. In addition to the roads, three groomed trails are available. Department of Natural Resources (DNR) sources recommend the Aspen Hills Trail, a 37-mile route that is accessed 5 miles west of U.S. Route 71 and State Highway 113. Buckboard Trail is 15.6 miles long, located 4 miles west of the town of Zerkel, reached via Lake Road off State Highway 37. Height of Land Trail is 19 miles long, accessible 15 miles west of U.S. Route 71 and State Highway 113.

Summer hikers enjoy trekking the Shuttlebug Nature Trail, two miles west of Zerkel. A state wildlife management area at Lower Rice Lake is just to the west, which means dozens of bird species can be spotted anytime of the day. Bring binoculars, sturdy walking boots, fruit juice, trail-mix snacks, and an interest in what is going on around you. It makes a great expedition for kids.

Where: White Earth State Forest sprawls across Mahnomen, Clearwater, and Becker Counties. The northeast unit of the forest is located in Clearwater County, just south of Bagley. Access is via State Highway 92, a roadway that forms the western border of the forest. The western unit is 20 miles east of Mahnomen, its forest carpet divided by State Highway 200. The southern unit is 20 miles east of Waubun.

For more information: Park Rapids Area Forest Supervisor, Box 113, 607 West First Street, Park Rapids, MN 56470. Call 218-732-3309; or Bemidji Area Forest Supervisor, 2220 Bemidji Avenue, Bemidji, MN 56601. Call 218-755-2890.

Pets: Best to leave at home, unless you have a hunting dog.
Leash them when they're not earning their keep.
Best time to visit: Year-round.
Activities: Hiking, fishing, hunting, trapping, fruit picking,
mushroom hunting, animal watching.

Tamarac National Wildlife Refuge

In the heart of Becker County, the Tamarac National Wildlife Refuge never seems to end. The bald eagles that live here
probably appreciate the remoteness, the space, the sharp skies.
If they could talk, they would tell you about what it means to
fly unhindered. The eagles appear in great numbers, beginning in April. The Tamarac has more of these stately birds
than all the other national wildlife refuges outside Alaska.
Logged over, the land was farmed for a time, but the bogs
won the race against the crops and most farmers abandoned
their plots by the 1930s. The empty fields quickly reverted
back to a more natural state as second-growth timber took
over. The 43,000-acre refuge was created in 1938 with the
sale of duck stamps, to protect the breeding grounds of migratory birds. The Civilian Conservation Corps built roads and
trails throughout the region, dotting the waysides with outbuildings and cabins.

You can visit most parts of the refuge throughout the year;
however, the midsection is open only seasonally to protect
nesting birds, and the northwest corner is a wilderness area
and off-limits. But you can go berry picking or mushroom
hunting and watch the birds to your heart's content. A visitors center at the refuge tells which areas are closed at any
particular time, so check in first before wandering out with
berry bucket in hand. Stand on the center's observation deck
overlooking the refuge for a good look at the wealth of

tamarack trees, which gives the place its name. A self-guided nature trail begins near the center, giving kids a perfect introduction to the wonders of the park interior. A five-mile cross-country ski trail wends its twisted, up-and-down way around Pine and Tamarac Lakes for a winter adventure.

It is also easy to tour by car, regardless of the weather. A leaflet provided at the visitors center traces the best routes to take along 10 miles of backcountry roadways that skirt the wetlands. If you're lucky, you may even see a rare trumpeter swan.

Where: The refuge is located 18 miles northeast of Detroit Lakes so drive east on State Highway 34, then turn north at Rochert on County Highway 29, which takes you to the refuge.

For more information: Park Manager, 35704 County Road 26, Rochert, MN 56578. Call 218-847-2641.

Pets: Leashed.

Activities: Hunting, fishing, boating, hiking, bird-watching, photography.

Zippel Bay State Park

There had to be a state park beginning with "Z" in Minnesota, to round out the alphabet-soup system. On the far northern side of the vast Lake of the Woods, which washes the shore of the park, is Mountie Country—Canada. The Minnesota-born author Tim O'Brien (of Worthington) used the name of the lake in his blockbuster 1994 novel entitled *In the Lake of the Woods.* In it, a Vietnam War veteran and Minnesota political leader and his wife vacation in the Lake of the Woods area. The woman disappears, shortly afterward followed by her husband. The book leaves the question open of what happened to both. The writer discusses secrets that each of us have in our relationships, in a setting of soughing pines, tannin-colored water, star-speckled nights, and sun-drenched days.

The lake makes a perfect backdrop for such a story. The vast body of water dominates the landscape in far northwestern Minnesota, stretching over 1,485 square miles, with 65,000 miles of shoreline and 14,000 islands. Lake of the Woods is 55 miles at its widest point and varies in depth from four feet to 35 feet at its southern end. The northern bays can be up to 150 feet deep. It is the perfect place in which to become lost, whether one does it willingly as an escape or the soul does it figuratively as a fugitive, as the talented O'Brien points out.

Visitors to Zippel are amazed at the changing moods of the lake. It can lull the guest with its glasslike surface, tickled only by the finger strokes of a western summer breeze. Or the water can rage and tear at itself with frenzied three-foot-high pre-winter waves, to explode its icy spray over the boulders lining the shore. The experienced weather watcher on the lake needs to be alert for quick atmospheric changes and must deal accordingly with a body of water that seemingly has a life and mind of its own.

One of the most interesting experiences in Zippel is trudging along the park shoreline, with its black-sand beaches formed from iron-ore flakes pulverized by wave action over thousands of years. Fanatic beachcombers, such as myself, can also find gnarled branches, shells, skin-smooth boulders, and other treasures washed up on the shoreline.

Inland there are many other natural riches: from the tangled mazes of berry patches to the secret pockets of edible mushrooms. The park is dotted with tiny clearings, where the dedicated, patient observer can watch deer, otter, beaver, black bear, pine marten, and other wildlife doing their northern Minnesota thing. Sometimes a moose is sighted, and the howling of wolves can be heard. The park landscape has a gentle feel to it, forested as it is and rolling and undulating like the waves offshore. There are numerous distinct, sharp slopes that mark the ancient borders of the lake. You can get one of the best views of Zippel Bay by climbing up the rocks next to the boat harbor and looking out over the mood-changing water. Whether you experience a hot July noon atop the granite outcropping or brave a teeth-chattering January wind, you'll realize that this lake has power beyond whatever you could have imagined while sitting in your armchair at home and reading this book.

Prehistoric people lived in this vicinity eons ago, ranging up and down the Rainy River. Several Native American nations, especially the Ojibway, Cree, Dakota, Monsonis, and Assiniboin, knew intimately the inlets and islands comprising the lake's environs. In 1732, Pierre Goultier de la Verendrye canoed the huge lake with 50 hardy men. Seeking sites for trading posts, he established a major camp at Fort St. Charles on what is now called Magnuson's Island in the so-called Northwest Angle of Lake of the Woods. From that camp the French branched out to open the frontier to other traders and trappers. Even when the British took control of the territory in 1763, voyageurs continued to ply these waters. For another 75 years, they hauled furs and goods back and forth from the wilds to the posts in their 26-foot-long birch-bark canoes.

The United States took possession of the area in 1783, after which followed almost half a century of arguments with Canada over the exact border through the wilderness. In 1887 William M. Zippel became one of the first whites to permanently settle at what is now Zippel Bay. By 1909 a large fishing village was in full swing, harvesting the giant sturgeon that lived in the murky lake depths. The sturgeon were estimated to be a century old, with some weighing up to 250 pounds. Occasionally fishermen today even catch one of these mighty fish. But don't bet on it being you. Such occurrences are very rare.

Zippel Bay State Recreation Area was legislated in 1959, comprising 2,766 acres. In 1963, recreational development of the park was commenced. Now there are 57 drive-in campsites, along with nature trails, a swimming beach (brrrrrr, cold water!), public boat harbor, fish-cleaning station, and trailer dump station. Snowmobile, cross-country, hiking, and horseback-riding trails loop through the pinelike spiderwebs.

The park is a haven for many rare species of birds and animals, little seen in more populated areas. Bird-watchers are free to go catatonic when spotting a piping plover, a small, white-and-brown shorebird. Only 50-some breeding individuals are known to inhabit the lake vicinity, nesting on Pine and Curry Islands near the southeast corner of the lake. Visitors to the park are asked to leave the birds alone.

If you find Tim O'Brien's hero and heroine on your explorations around Zippel Bay State Park, let the rest of his fans know. We've been dying to learn the secret of the Lake of the Woods.

Where: The park is 10 miles northeast of Williams on the shore of Lake of the Woods. Entrance to the park is from Lake of the Woods County State Aid Highway 8.

For more information: Zippel Bay State Park, Box 25, Williams, MN 56686. Call 218-783-6252.

Amenities: Here's a fishing tip from state forest folks who know what it is all about when it comes to angling. On sticky afternoons in May, June, and July, use a leech or nightcrawler on a slip sinker near the bottom, in water ranging from eight to 30 feet in depth. You are almost guaranteed to land a keeper that might even include a sauger, a distant relative of the walleye. 'Nuff said on that. For any more tips, you can hire your own guide. Firewood is available for sale at park headquarters, so leave the downed wood alone. Nearby resorts have ice for sale, with gas and groceries available at several stations about eight miles east of the park entrance. Area resorts regularly host day or half-day fishing expeditions for walleye and northern pike.

Pets: Leashed.

Best time to visit: Summer, autumn.

Activities: Swimming, hiking, boating, horseback riding, fishing, camping, snowmobiling, sightseeing.

Other: Every year the park offers a specialized interpretive program around which various talks and demonstrations concentrate. They can focus on a particular species; land use, watershed, and environmental concerns; or some other topic. Check the park headquarters for programs.

2

Northeast

M innesota's Arrowhead Country is a sharpened flint
pointing out from the upper northeast corner of the
state. On a map Cook County is the tip of that arrowhead.
You won't get much more remote than by standing near the
Grand Portage National Monument, at the far end of a skinny,
rocky peninsula jutting into Lake Superior. Traffic scoots past
on U.S. Route 61, but the land outside the monument border
lies within the Grand Portage Indian Reservation, which in
turn is backed up to the west by the Grand Portage State Forest. The national monument, marking the first white settlement in Minnesota, is only a mile or so from the Canadian
border.

Trapper/trader laVerendrye set up camp there in 1731 with
a hardy band of muscled, mustachioed French Canadians who
viewed this wilderness as a treasure trove, one brimming with
economic opportunities. The site soon became the jumping-
off point for a well-known *voyageurs'* portage from Lake
Superior to Fort Charlotte and points farther west. From the
vantage point of the national monument, facing you to the
east are 31,000 square miles of chilly, rolling Lake Superior
waters, considered variously as "Gitchee-goome" (the Big
Waters), by Native Americans; "the ship eater," by storm-
tossed sailors; or "the most magical, magnificent spread of
sparkling fresh water in the world, an unparalleled natural

resource," by enthusiastic tourism promoters. They are all correct.

With the signing of the Treaty of LaPointe in 1854 with the Lake Superior Ojibway bands, much of northern and eastern Minnesota was opened to white settlement. Prospectors were the first to stampede in, seeking gold and iron ore. By the 20th century, the region was freckled with mines. Next came the loggers who took almost everything remaining of living, growing, natural value by the time of World War I. The land was cut over or burned off, with the resulting image of a desolate moonscape. However, the Superior National Forest had been established in 1909 to protect what little was being spared by the loggers' saws. Enlightened locals wanted some of the wilderness preserved for recreational uses. As a result of their lobbying, 1,000 square miles of remaining timber were set aside in 1926 as a "wilderness recreational area," with more land added in the 1930s. This Superior Roadless Area was renamed the Boundary Waters Canoe Area (BWCA) in 1958. The Wilderness Act of 1964 designated the area as a unit of the National Wilderness Protection System. New laws established a mining protection area, ended all timber harvesting, and gave the region the contemporary title of Boundary Waters Canoe Area Wilderness (BWCAW).

Along with the BWCAW, the Superior National Forest, and several state parks and forests, northeastern Minnesota is also gateway to the rugged Isle Royale National Park (under Michigan's jurisdiction), the home of wolves and moose. The island is offshore from the town of Grand Portage via a 90-minute ferryboat ride.

Back on land some of the nation's best outdoor recreation opportunities can be found in the neighboring forests here, accessed off the Arrowhead, Gunflint, Caribou, and Sawbill Trails. Don't get the impression that these are narrow trails through the woods. They are the primary roads maintained to link resorts, campsites, pine plantations, crossroad taverns, and canoe launchings.

Whatever the season, this far outpost of Minnesota provides perfect *au naturel* getaways. Spring, with its fresh forest blooms and new life everywhere, and heat-soaked summers are perfect for muscle-stretching hiking and biking, along with "glad-I-ain't-at-work" fishing for lunker pike and bass. If walking, be prepared for thigh-stretching climbs. Even the sturdiest boots will show wear and tear, making each night's camp a welcome relief. And have rain gear close at hand.

My favorite season, however, is always autumn, regardless of the weather's vagaries. A motorist can meander down any of the 394 miles of country roads specially marked for color tours, taking in the blazing maples and oaks and soaking up the air's sharp pre-snow snap. The Native Americans believed that ancient star hunters killed the sky-dwelling Great Bear. Its dripping blood changed some of the leaves red, and the fat spattered from its cooking meat made other leaves yellow. Of course, the tried-and-true Jack Frost story works just as well. Actually the trees stop manufacturing green chlorophyll as the days shorten, which allows other pigments to take over. But that scientific touch takes the North Woods romance away. So just enjoy the thousands of square miles laid out in quilt-colorful profusion and don't worry about the whys of it all.

The first colorama season begins when the hardwood forests proudly show off their stuff. Peak season for the maples and oaks is generally between September 20 and October 10. For the second show, the aspen, birch, and poplar go on stage with a crimson backdrop of blazing sumac to set the tone. This act usually peaks between October 5 and 20. Motels, hotels, and many campsites fill up quickly, especially on weekends during the autumn viewing as motorcoaches and autos migrate northward. Plan your time accordingly when seeking rooms. And be aware that snow flurries are often spotted by mid-October, but you won't need a snow shovel until November. Temperatures hover in the 50s and 60s during the day and fall to the 20s and 30s at night. Dress in layers for the weather; you can always peel off a sweatshirt if it becomes too warm, whether you paddle a canoe or sit on a cabin porch.

Now some insights for the winter, which is certainly glacial in imagery: icicles, drifts up to the nose, scudding gray clouds, roaring winds around the cabin eaves, snow-draped pine boughs. That has never bothered rugged Minnesotans, who just slip on an extra-heavy pair of mittens and then hit the crisp air. After all there are more than 300 miles of cross-country ski trails to explore, plus ice skating, sledding, winter camping, and snowmobiling to give a wonderful edge to the year's frostiest season. Who wants to waste all that! There are also enough organized North Country outdoor activities to fill any dance card. The John Beargrease Sled Dog Marathon with its 500-mile marathon, the Jeep 500 Snowmobile Race, and the Sawtooth Mountain 25K Cross-Country Ski Race are among the events pulling in top national competitors.

But don't think that only top amateurs and pros can have a good time in the North Country. Novice and intermediate skiers are always welcome, even if they wear jeans tucked into high wool socks instead of sleek speed gear. Traditional diagonal skiing is prevalent along trails in the Lake Superior area, but ski-skating lanes are located at the Bally Creek area, between the Caribou Trail (County Highway 4) and Solbakken Resort, and above the Oberg Mountain parking lot on County Road 336. Trails are always groomed at least weekly in single-track fashion, with ski-skating lanes alongside the regular trail in designated sections. Depending on the amount of measurable snowfall, tracking crews are in the woods immediately.

The 170-mile North Shore State Trail is primarily a snow-mobile run from Duluth to Grand Marais over rugged coun-tryside with its mixed forest, numerous streams, and rivers. Along the way you'll pass Gooseberry Falls, Split Rock Light-house, Baptism River, George H. Crosby Manitou, Temper-ance River, and Cascade River State Parks. Traversing St. Louis, Lake, and Cook Counties, many scenic overlooks offer smashingly great views of the sluggish ice-clogged waters of blue-black Lake Superior. The trail can also be used by warm-weather bikers, as well as riders, taking advantage of 50 miles of horseback trails scattered at various points along the route.

Don't get the idea that northeastern Minnesota is at the end of the world, decorated only with thousands of miles of maple trees and inhabited by pine martens and blue jays. There are towns, complete with community theaters, art gal-leries, pizza parlors, golf courses, grand resorts, and all the other accoutrements of civilization. Grand Marais jokes that it is the seat of the Scandinavian Riviera, due to the over-whelmingly Nordic population. With only 1,200 permanent residents, the area hosts more than 4,500 visitors in the sum-mer on any given day. Don't worry about overcrowding how-ever. Most are passing through on their way to bike or hike. Ely, "The Canoe Capital of the World," offers some of the best access to the bwcaw. And you have to visit the Interna-tional Wolf Center there to observe and learn about these amazing animals. The facility is open daily from 9:00 a.m. to 5:30 p.m. from May 1 to October 31 and from 10:00 a.m. to 5:00 p.m. Friday, Saturday, and Sunday from November 1 to April 31. The center is closed Christmas Day. Admission is $5.50 for adults and teens, $5.00 for seniors, and free for chil-dren under six. The center has numerous exhibits and pro-grams, as well as field trips, wolf-survey expeditions, and tracking projects in the wilderness. Take the family on a wolf-howling trip (call for rates). Participants meet at the center for a presentation on wolf communication. You then head out into the deep woods with a naturalist who can actually howl up a pack. It's a real spine-tingler . . . and totally safe. Call 800-ELY-WOLF for hours other than in the summer.

Where: The International Wolf Center is located at 1396 Highway 169, Ely, MN, 55731-8129.

For more information: Superior National Forest & Boundary Waters Canoe Area Wilderness, Box 338, Duluth, MN 55801. Call 218-720-5324 (for camping reservations, call 218-720-5440); Grand Marais Chamber of Commerce. Call 800-622-4014 or 218-387-2524; Grand Portage Information Center, Box 307, Grand Portage, MN 55605. Call 800-232-1385 (from Canada, call 800-543-1384); Tip of the Arrowhead Association, Box 1048, Grand Marais, MN 55604. Call 800-622-4014 or 218-387-2524; Gunflint Trail Association, Box 205, Grand Marais, MN 55604. Call 800-338-6932. Website: www.gunflint-trail.com.

Pets: Leash 'em or leave 'em.

Activities: Hiking, biking, snowmobiling, horseback riding, fishing, swimming, photography, loafing, reading, and of course relaxing.

Boundary Waters Canoe Area Wilderness

The fabled BWCAW stretches for 150 miles along the Minnesota–Ontario border, with its several thousand lakes and streams linked by portages within the quarter-million-acre park. Motorboats are *verboten* on all but a few of the waterways. Within the federally protected reserve, you won't find any stores or roads, although the area is ringed by numerous resorts, campgrounds, and other accommodations. "Carry-in, carry-out." That's the motto for BWCAWers. A dozen outfitters service guests, providing everything from canoes to camp stoves.

Where: Since the BWCAW is so spread out, there are more than 70 entry points throughout the Cook/Crane Lake, Ely, Tofte, Isabella, and Grand Marais areas. For instance around Grand Marais, there are at least 32 places in which to launch a canoe for overnight tripping and another five for day-use visitors. Check local maps for specifics.

For more information: Voyageurs National Park, 3131 Highway 53, International Falls, MN 56649. Call 218-283-9821. Ely Outfitters Association, Box 788, Ely, MN 55731.

Pets: Leave 'em in the kennel.

Best times to visit: The BWCAW is most used on the opening weekend of fishing season, holiday weekends, and from mid-July through the first three weeks of August. Consider a trip starting midweek, rather than on a weekend, to avoid the crush around the boat landings. In late May, September, and early October, few bugs will be out to bother you. This is a welcome relief to anyone familiar with Minnesota's bomber-size mosquitoes. Remember that the BWCAW is the most heavily used wilderness in the nation, although most times you would never know it because of the vast distances between camps and canoeists.

Activities: Fishing, canoeing, houseboating, cross-country skiing.

Other: Campgrounds are free on a first-come first-served basis. A limited number of permits are subsequently issued each day for the 100 entry points. Every overnight party and day-use motor party of up to nine persons must have a permit in a member's possession while within the park from May to September. Day hikers and paddlers do not need a permit. You can get a permit by reserving ahead of time or on a walk-in basis if any are available (it's not worth the chance to wait until the last minute, so take advantage of the reservations). Canoe outfitters can also secure permits for their guests. For more details call the Rainy Lake Visitor Center, 218-286-5258.

Cascade River State Park

Lake Superior was gray-green black, with a hand-chilling numbness. Waves roiled against the moss-covered, slimy breakwater rocks that were piled along the waterfront to disperse the surf. The waves snarled and foamed, creeping up toward the land and falling back exhausted, only to try again and again. Seven-year-old Dan stuck his head out of the tent, only to gasp in the frosty October breeze before pulling back inside. His thick red hair was tousled with sleep and he shivered before snuggling back in the sleeping bag for one last grateful yawn. We were on our way northward to a late autumn camping, fishing, and four-wheel-drive expedition deep into the Tofte region of the Superior National Forest, pausing at Cascade River for an overnight.

Even the gas tent heater wasn't enough to ward off the cold, augmented by the blustery wind from over the lake. Our canvas rattled all night as all the elements of Minnesota seemingly tried to crawl through the zippered front flap. Layers of thermal hinder binders, stocking caps, and heavy pajamas probably kept us from a dramatic Jack London death. "Are we gonna be frozen stiff by tomorrow, Dad?" Dan had asked plaintively before huddling deep down in his sleeping bag the night before. Obviously, however, he was tougher than he had expected and survived, at least long enough to greet the unsmiling, red dawn as the sun clawed up from the eastern horizon.

Morning, even in the cold pre-winter, hurriedly arrives at Cascade River. A breakfast of fried, easy-over eggs and jam-laden toasted muffins, grilled on the cookstove and washed down with milk, had followed a generally loud splashing of wake-up water on faces and other hastily exposed body parts. It's amazing the human sounds that are made when ice-crimped water hits the epidermis. More than one moose in the backcountry was probably startled by the whoops. So by the time breakfast was ready, Dan's pink face glowed like the sunrise. Dishes cleaned, grounds policed, tent struck, truck loaded—ah, warm again. We were ready to face the next challenge. And it was only 7:24 A.M.

Both the campgrounds and the picnic area along U.S. Route 61 provide a close-up, albeit windy, vantage point to pull over and observe the monster lake in all its daily excitement—regardless of the season. Every day, the view to the east is different, ever changing as the Sybillike moods of the lake switch from calm to fierce.

The park stretches its thin finger for one and a half miles along the shoreline on both sides of the highway, the main route to Canada. Only about a half mile deep, Cascade River snuggles up against red-pine plantings and maples of the Superior National Forest, which rears out of the hills to the west. The park is midway between the crossroads village of Lutsen on the south and Grand Marais, the outfitting capital of Minnesota, on the north.

Covering 2,813 acres, the park is one of the most diverse in northeastern Minnesota: shoreline, rivers, creeks, forests. The geology of the landscape was formed about a billion years ago when the bedrock was swallowed by a sea of molten lava from ancient volcanoes. Next a vast shallow ocean flooded North America, dumping sediment over the by-now cold lava beds. Erosion and glaciers added their creative touches during the creation of the contemporary Lake Superior basin. Today the sculpting actions of water, wind, and rain, along with alternating freezing and thawing, are still at work making new shapes.

For photos try your hand at landscapes along the Cascade River, especially Cascade Falls, which can be reached from the campgrounds. A picnic shelter also overlooks the mist-shrouded falls, a series of drops that range over a mile carrying the water over a 225-foot incline. Another good walk is up to the peak of Lookout Mountain, 500 feet above Lake Superior. The strenuous hike begins about a mile into the national forest. Be sure to take along your fly rod and creel because the brook trout in the Cascade River are super.

The Jonvik deer yard is the largest winter deer yard in Minnesota, accommodating hundreds of animals at a time. The thick stands of trees ringing the yard offer protection from the wind and cold, even when Canada lobs its howlers out of the north every winter. Looking back, Dan figured that would have been the place to stay on our expedition. You might even spot some moose along Indian Camp or Cutface Creek. It's not likely, however, because the animals are very skittish and hide in the deep woods. But surprises happen. Stay in your car if one crunches out of the forest near a roadway. If hiking, remain away from the big beasts if you see one. Wolves and fishers are also area residents, with the expansive national forest as their playground.

Where: Cascade State Park is located in Minnesota's Cook County, only nine miles southwest of Grand Marais. Drive along U.S. Route 61 northeast out of Tofte for 21 miles to the information center in the park.
For more information: Cascade River State Park Manager,

3481 West Highway 61, Lutsen, MN 55612-9535. Call 218-387-3053.

Hours: The park is closed from 10:00 P.M. to 8:00 A.M., except to registered campers.

Amenities: There are 40 semimodern campsites with showers and flush toilets and a year-round shelter building with four picnic tables, woodstove, and electricity. There are also five backpack campsites, 18 miles of hiking trails, 17 miles of cross-country ski trails, 2 miles of snowmobile trails, and seven picnic sites along Lake Superior. The trails were built by the Civilian Conservation Corps in the 1930s and remain in excellent shape. In the winter snowmobile trails are groomed by the Cook County Ridge Riders and the Lutsen Trailbreakers, ensuring a pleasant and safe trip.

Pets: Leashed.

Best time to visit: Anytime (just dress for the weather).

Activities: Hiking, snowmobiling, snowshoeing, camping, picnicking, fishing, mountain biking.

Others: Due to the thick forests, be sure to build fires only in designated areas, with wood available for purchase from the camp staff. However, portable stoves and grills are permitted.

Gunflint Trail

The 63 miles of the paved Gunflint Trail (County Road 12) lie on the eastern end of the Boundary Waters Canoe Area Wilderness. The road begins in Grand Marais and is the prime access route to the BWCAW, the Superior National Forest, and Quetico Park in Canada. Traffic is most heavy in midsummer, but you can still stop to hear the cry of a wolf on star-struck nights. Consider the Gunflint as merely an artery to get you to where the action is, whether for cycling, fishing, canoeing, or winter sports.

Members of the Gunflint Trail Association, the confeder-
ation of resort owners, B&B operators, outfitters, and other
service vendors are eager to help long-time visitors or first-
timers. Use 'em. Sue McDonnell, spokesperson for the association, operates the Dreamcatcher B&B in Grand Marais
with her husband, Jack. Although visually impaired, Jack
McDonnell has never been one to sit still. He's out and about
all the time and will offer plenty of tips on what can be
accomplished even if there are some physical challenges for
outdoor lovers. Others, such as Dave and Barb Tuttle, who
have run the Bearskin Lodge and Cross Country Ski Resort
since 1973, are among the old-timers who know the value of
vacations. "They are important to me," said Dave Tuttle. "So
I want my guests to receive what I insist on," he emphasized.
Everyone has a story. Charlet and Bud Kratoskas have owned
Trout Lake Resort since 1945 and built up their property from
one boathouse and a cabin into a modern seven-unit facility.
Terry Parson's main lodge on Hungry Jack Lake burned down
in 1972, shortly after he purchased the circa-1924 building. He
found another log structure in Grand Marais and moved it
log by log to his property, restored it to its original finish, and
lifted everything back into place with lots of sweat and hard
work.

Here's something different: a yurt ski adventure along the
25-kilometer Banadad tracked trail. Each yurt, a peaked-roof
Mongolian tent, is staffed by a hut host who cooks and takes
care of the chores. There's hardly anything that can top a
Mongolian fire pot dinner: A fondue of veggies and meat is
cooked over charcoal and served with rice. Or maybe there'll
be grilled rainbow trout. Call Barb or Ted Young at Boundary County Trekking for all the scoop at 800-322-8327.

Several of the top canoe-only lakes are Moss, Vegetable,
Portage, Missing Link, and Ham. If you're wondering where
to find the fish, skilled guides are available on most waters. But

if skiing is your forte, rather than angling, the November-to-April cross-country season is top-notch. The Gunflint Lake Area Nordic Ski Trails Association has a Kassbauer Piston-Bully groomer out daily to make sure it stays that way on the 100-kilometer system. The region, which abuts Canada, averages 120 inches of snow annually. Two short trails are available for night skiing around Gunflint Lake. The better trails in the area are the Big Pine, South Rim, Magnetic Rock, East End, River, and Rabbit Run. Each is easy enough for beginners and intermediates, but challenging in distance. There's something else around Gunflint Lake: The folks have added a snowmobile-drawn cutter for a dash across the north shore of the lake into Canada. The sleigh takes you into the stomping grounds of a wolf pack.

Where: By car drive northeast from Duluth along the north shore of Lake Superior on U.S. Route 61 to Grand Marais. Then turn inland on County Highway 12—that's the trail. Plan on a three-hour drive.

For more information: Grand Marais Convention and Visitors Bureau, Box 1048, Grand Marais, MN 55604. Call 218-387-1400 or 888-922-5002. Website: www.grandmarais.com.

Pets: Leashed (but check individual resorts for policies; some ask that Fido and Kitty Cat be kept at home).

Best time to visit: Year-round.

Activities: Hiking, cycling, snowshoeing, cross-country skiing, hot-tub wallowing, fishing.

Lutsen–Tofte Area

A favorite ski destination for Minnesotans since the region was opened to such organized sports in 1948, the Lutsen–Tofte district of northeastern Minnesota has an extensive array of downhill and cross-country possibilities. With its vertical rise of 800 feet, the Lutsen Mountains are among the highest in the Midwest. Served by gondola and three chair lifts, up to 600 skiers an hour can be accommodated. There are also chalets, a ski school, and area restaurants catering to the downhillers. In 1995 the mountain's facilities underwent the second year of a five-year, million-dollar-plus development that includes adding ski runs and remodeling a chalet at the base of the slope. A high-speed chair lift and five expert chutes on the north face of Moose Mountain are next. There's no need to pack a lunch because the Mountain Top Deli and Restaurant atop the towering Moose serves up light lunches.

But for readers wishing a more relaxed pace along Minnesota's Lake Superior shore around Lutsen and Tofte, there are hundreds of miles of cross-country ski trails. More than $100,000 has been spent on trail improvements between 1992 and 1996, according to Bill Blank of Solbakken Resort. Wider bridges have been installed throughout the system, making it easier for passing.

One of the best ways to see the landscape is via the Lutsen Gondola, which slides off at treetop level from the Poplar River Valley and climbs upward to Moose Mountain. A blanket of pine, maple, oak, and aspen—whether in spring's fresh budding; summer's green; autumn's crimson, orange, and ochre; or winter's whipped-cream topping—spreads underneath the gently swaying car as far as the eye can see. The eight-minute ride costs $8.75 for adults, $7.75 for seniors 62 and older, and $5.75 for kids seven to 12. Four persons can be accommodated in each gondola, so toss your skis or mountain bikes aboard and save a walking trip.

Mountain Biking. A trail pass including a gondola ride is $12.00; a trail pass including unlimited gondola access is $18.00. Bike rentals are $24.00 for a full day of careening down the hills. There is a choice of trails from the top of Moose Mountain, starting in the intermediate range and progressing to advanced trails that even Herculo the Circus Wonder Cyclist may wonder why the heck he decided to plummet down them. There's plenty of open ledge rock for white-knuckled descents on which to test your balancing and riding skills. The five-and-three-fifths-mile Yellow Trail is probably (okay, it is!) the toughest with its wet areas, steep downhills, and alternating ascents. You start out calmly enough on the White Trail, the easiest portion of the system, which traverses the ridgeline of Moose Mountain. That six-and-three-tenths-mile run, which opened in 1995, is aimed mostly at beginners. But the more advanced cyclists can then spin off at the 1,550-foot elevation on the big Y.T. for the ride of their lives, one definitely not recommended for the faint of heart.

For mountain-biking fans take in the Lutsen Mountain Bike Festival held the last full weekend in June or the Moose Mountain MTB Classic, a cross-country race held each September. Both events take in all levels of experience.

Hiking. All the hiking trails in the Lutsen–Tofte area hover in the number-10 range. Challenging, rugged enough to be fun, scenic, with an abundance of wildlife, campsites/resorts, and accessibility combine to make a trekking experience here among the best in North America. Walking excursions can range from the quarter-mile Cross River Trail (access at the Cross River wayside rest area on U.S. Route 61) for an easy, slow climb to an excellent view of the river gorge to the 18 miles of the Cascade River Trail (access from Cascade State Park, U.S. Route 61). Several other fine trails are along the Temperance River, to the top of Carlton Peak via the Sawbill Trail Road, and the Oberg and Leveaux Mountain National Recreation Trails. Hikers will appreciate the wildflower interpretive guide found at the trail head at the parking lot off Forest Service Road 336.

Be sure to wear strong boots or rugged jogging shoes with nonskid soles because of the roller-coaster landscape that can be slippery when damp. Experienced hikers in these parts carry food and water as well as a first-aid kit, compass, and detailed maps for longer hikes. Although most of the trails are well marked and laid out, allow about two miles per hour for a vigorous workout.

A good, general map of Cook County's trails through the eastern Superior National Forest can be obtained from the Superior Hiking Trail Association, Box 4, Two Harbors, MN 55616. Call 218-834-2700. Detailed maps are available at ranger stations, resorts, and businesses throughout the vicinity.

Skiing. Lodge-to-lodge skiing is the freshest way to get an expanded look at what the Lake Superior shoreline has to offer in the winter. Packages are available from Sunday through Thursday during nonholiday times. Three- to five-night plans are available. Plan on spending $51.00 to $500.00 a night per person, double occupancy; this includes lodging, trail lunch, shuttle service, and tax. Among the resorts that are in the plan are Stone Hearth Inn, Fenstad's Resort, Bluefin Bay on Lake Superior, Cobblestone Cabins, Chateau Leveaux, Lutsen Resort and Sea Villas, Village Inn and Resort, Lindgren's B&B, Cascade Lodge & Restaurant, Solbakken Resort, Thomsonite Beach Motel, Track Outfitting, The Mountain Inn and Eagle Ridge.

Fireplaces, kitchens, pools, and saunas can be had at some places, while others such as Bear Track, don't have in-room phones or television to guarantee stress-free getaways. The facilities stretch along a 25-mile section of the lake, with from 5- to 11-mile jumps between each place. Your luggage will be delivered to the next stop in time for your arrival. This is certainly a relief and beats hauling a suitcase on your back over the mountains. The larger ski tour centers offer shuttle service to trailheads for guests, as well as rentals, waxing, instructions, and maps. A list can be secured from the tourism association.

Four-Wheel Driving. "Yahoo!" The panel truck bounded into the creek, slamming off the rocky bottom like a Ping-Pong ball. Water splashed against the windshield. We were cruising the Tofte area on service roads deep inside the Superior National Forest, mere pathways that had shock-killer written all over them. "For somebody not used to off-road driving or driving along washboard gravel roads, the first time into the woods can be a surprise and unsettling," Assistant Ranger Terry Eggum had said earlier, as we checked in to tell of our driving plans. Trim in his green-gray work clothes, he looked snug and secure behind his desk in the Tofte Forest Service station. Yet out in the boonies, his words rang clear as the Vatican's bells.

Wife Sandy, oldest son Dan, and I were camping at Crescent Lake Campgrounds, about 25 miles inland from Lake Superior, eating beans instead of hoped-for fish because it was late October. The walleye were feeling the change of seasons and avoiding our lures. So it was put the poles away and head into the woods on a moose hunt—armed with camera of course. Loggers we met kept saying, "Sure, enough. A cow and bull went through here yesterday." The men were right. Fresh washtub-size hoofprints were spotted along many of the narrow back roads ringing the multitudinous tamarack swamps dotting the region. No real moose were seen, however. The 1,500-pound-plus critters are hard to miss.

Driving the forest roads is better than an amusement park flume plunge when the air is crisp, the leaves are turning, and imagined moose perfume is in the breeze. Before you go, be sure your vehicle is built and equipped for the backcountry cruising: tires in good shape, plenty of gas, chains, lanterns, food, water, and sleeping bags. Always stay on marked trails because wide tires can rip up the shallow ground cover and cause horrendous erosion problems on what is actually a fragile ecosystem. There is plenty of macho or "femino" challenge in downshifting, jouncing through potholes, climbing up 45-degree slopes, grinding through mountain streams—all on "improved" roads—without resorting to ripping up the landscape on your own. Among the best we found was Forest Service Road 384, which cuts along the rim of Whitefish Lake. Thick pucker brush hinders driving, as do branches bent over from heavy snow during the previous winters. Experienced drivers keep a sharp brush hook in the back seat for such emergencies because it beats backing up several hundred feet before a turnaround exit can be found. Then there was FSR 357 from Harry Creek to the junction with FSR 1224, another bouncing bottom bruiser (wear seat belts!) as you crawl through the bumper-deep angry waters of Wilson Creek. You just rev and roar through ... bang! ... oof! ... to hit the boulders that are called "road" on the opposite bank for the next neck-jerking uphill climb. The rewards from surviving such white-knuckled timber driving are numerous: Cecil B. deMille scenic overlooks, maybe a moose or bear sighting, satisfaction of knowing that you made it through alive without a broken axle. The mountains can win, you know, and it is a long hike out for help.

Where: Tofte is about 65 miles north of Duluth on U.S. Route 61. The picturesque jaunt extends for about another 20 miles along the Lake Superior shoreline to Lutsen.
For more information: Lutsen–Tofte Tourism Association, Box 2248, Tofte, MN 55615. Call 218-663-7804 or 888-61-NORTH.

Pets: Keep on a leash or leave at home, especially in the winter.
Best time to visit: Year-round.
Activities: Skiing, snowmobiling, hiking, camping, bird-watching, picnicking, colorama tours, backcountry driving.

Superior Hiking Trail

The Superior Hiking Trail links seven state parks and county and U.S. Forest Service roads, offering numerous trailheads. The 200 miles of completed trails run from Two Harbors to the Canadian border, with an unfinished connection of 20 miles from Duluth to Two Harbors. Trail officials hope that by the year 2000 that section will also be finalized. "We started in the middle and built out," said Tricia Ryan, executive director of the Superior Hiking Trail Association. Originally from Duluth, Ryan started out with a degree in design, then became a trail volunteer and grew into the director's position by 1989. The organization now has 1,500 members from throughout the country, and even one member from Scotland.

The accessibility of the trail, with access points every five to 10 miles, makes it great for day hiking, according to Ryan. Each walk is rugged and often difficult but always rewarding for the view. "There is such a variety in what you hike through, from river valleys to dramatic overlooks over Lake Superior and inland lakes. It's a 'like wow!' trail. The Superior takes people by surprise because it's so well maintained and well signed. It's the best of all worlds for the hiker," Ryan continued. I certainly agree that the Superior is the Cadillac of wilderness trails.

The state legislature gave money to the nonprofit association to build and maintain the system, with construction going on from 1987 through 1993. You can pick up the trailhead in Two Harbors at Silver Creek Township Road 613, four miles north of town on U.S. Route 61. The concluding point is at Jackson Lake Road, north of the town of Hovland, about 15 miles north of Grand Marais. The trail will eventually go straight north of Hovland to Canada.

Maps of the existing system are available for 50 cents each, although the trail is well marked with wood-routed signage at trailheads and three-inch by four-inch plastic signs mounted on cedar blocks tacked to trees. Bears have damaged some signs while marking out their territories, but they are afraid of humans and usually fade quickly into the berry patches when someone comes near. Just be warned, however, when spring-time cubs are present that Ma Bear isn't any playroom teddy. She will quickly rise to defend her brood against any per-ceived threat. To a bear, perception is reality, so stay clear.

The four-pack of maps covers Two Harbors to Tette-gouche, Tettegouche to Oberg Mountain, Oberg Mountain to Woods Creek, and Woods Creek to Canada. Some of the best moose sightings along the system are from Jackson Lake Road off the Arrowhead Trail, under the shadow of Far-quhuar Peak. Or you can park your car near Carlson Creek on the Arrowhead or at the Jackson Lake Road crossing of the Superior Hiking Trail. Trek inland and sweep your eyes across the tamarack swamps to the north. Several of the big beasts can often be spotted wallowing in the marshland. Good bear habitat is along Palisade Creek inside Tettegouche State Park, and you can always spot turkey vultures and porcupines in the vicinity.

The trail crosses many major and minor creeks, all of which are bridged. The physically challenged can also make their way along the system. Witness the efforts of Paul Hlina of Superior, whose brace and crutches from a spinal-cord injury didn't keep him from trekking 200 miles along the trail in three weeks in the summer of 1995.

"But since the system is tough for anybody, we don't promote it as handicap accessible," said Ryan.

The trail consists of about an 18-inch walkway, in a four-foot-wide clearing through jack pine and maple. At its lowest point, the trail is 602 feet above sea level and 1,829 feet above Lake Superior at its highest.

Where: The trailhead is located at Two Harbors on Silver Creek Township Road 613, four miles north of town on U.S. Route 61.

Amenities: Hikers are encouraged to take a one-way shuttle on the Superior Hiking Trail. You can park your car at the end point of your hike and catch the scheduled shuttle that takes you to the trailhead you request. You can then hike back to your car. Rates are $7.00 for adults. The cost is $4.00 per additional trailhead. The service runs every Friday, Saturday, and Sunday from late May to mid-October. It also runs the Mondays of Memorial Day and Labor Day weekends and on the Fourth of July holiday weekend. For more information contact Dan Sanders, Superior Shuttle, 960 Highway 61 East, Two Harbors, MN 55616. Call 218-834-5511.

There are no permit regulations concerning camping along the trail. Any campsites are available on a first-come, first-served basis, and all are free except within a state park. The sites offer latrines, fire rings, water sources, and tent areas. Be sure to boil or chemically treat water however. If a campsite is full, hikers can settle down in the Superior National Forest as long as it is not posted and is at least 100 feet from a water source and the trail itself.

Other: The Superior Hiking Trail Association publishes a five-times-a-year newsletter, *The Ridgeline*, which is packed with information and stories about programs, members, and services. Memberships are $25.00 for individuals; $35.00 per family; $15.00 for students; $100.00 for a basic business membership; $500.00 for lifetime memberships; and $40.00 for associations, youth groups, and nonprofit corporations. For specifics contact the association at Box 4, Two Harbors, MN 55616-0004. Call 218-834-2700. Contributions for maintenance, bridge work, and other trail improvements are tax deductible. The association's office and a store are in Two Harbors. Office hours are from 9:00 A.M. to 5:00 P.M. Monday through Friday, with extended hours during the summer hiking season. You can also purchase T-shirts and fanny packs, as well as other premiums and trail guides. The buildings are on U.S. Route 61 in Two Harbors at the corner of Seventh Avenue.

Superior National Forest

If you ever wanted to see trees, lakes, and mountains, the Superior National Forest is the place for sensory overload. More than three million acres of pine, water, and rock form the roof of Minnesota. Created by volcanic activity 700 million years ago and polished by subsequent glacial activity, this ancient landscape offers superb hiking, hunting, birdwatching, fishing, dogsledding, biking, snowmobiling, kayaking, and a round of other outdoor adventures.

I've taken the Sawtooth Trail on four-by-four driving adventures and camped in the forest. The Sawtooth, one of the major roads traversing the forest, was once a footpath that connected Tofte's North Shore Ranger Station with the lookout tower at Sawbill Lake in the 1920s. The first two and a half miles of what was once trail is now a paved highway, with the remainder a gravel road. Along the way you can see the sites of old Civilian Conservation Corps camps, a white-pine blister rust test area (surrounded by a moose-proof fence), the vestiges of an old railroad bed used by loggers, and the Lyght homestead near Caribou Lake. The latter is interesting because the Lyghts were the first African-American family to settle in this predominately Norwegian-Swedish area. One of the 13 Lyght children was sheriff of Cook County in the mid-1990s.

Mountain biking is one of the most fun ways of seeing the Superior National Forest, if you want to cover more distance quicker than hiking. The Timber/Frear/Cross Lake Trail is a 30 mile challenge over a mostly hard gravel surface, some of it unintentionally washboarded to shake out the kinks. While Forest Service Roads 346 and 357 are reasonably well surfaced, you will run into rocks, potholes, and pucker brush thick enough to knock off your helmet on FSR 347 and 348. Timber, Elbow, Finger, Whitefish, and Fourmile Lakes can be seen on this route. Access is via parking lots near any of the gravel pits in the area (at the intersection of Forest Service Roads 170/357 and 170/1226) or at well-marked boat-launch sites. Take FSR 343, just south of Tofte, to its intersection with 166, turn left to pick up FSR 346 or right to 344. For a different challenge, try the ski trails that are unused in the summer. Although they can be mushy after a rain and covered with high grass, you won't encounter many other bikers, especially on the Sugarbush Trail. The 17-mile loop is reached via County Highway 2 about an eighth of a mile north of Tofte.

Two good biking trails are just south of the Boundary Waters Canoe Area Wilderness. One is the 20-mile Lime Mountain run over hard gravel. Connecting several lakes, the ride takes you past a number of clear lakes, across the Brule River, and through some lovely pine forests. Access one route at the intersection of County Highway 12 and FSR 315, which ends at the East/West Twin Lake Campgrounds on FSR 152. Another biking trail is off County Highway 12 on County

Highway 66, a soft-surfaced, six-mile run that edges over ridges and into shallow valleys, ending at Clearwater Lake. An abandoned railroad grade picked up at the lake provides a quicker return. Be sure not to bike on the Superior Hiking Trail.

Where: Duluth, headquarters of the Superior National Forest, is 60 miles south of the sprawling timberland. The city is reached via bus, plane, and I-35 from the Twin Cities. Daily bus service from Duluth, provided by the Northern Transportation Company, takes travelers to towns within the forest boundaries. Three primary roadways access the forest: State Highway 61 runs parallel to the Lake Superior shoreline; U.S. Route 53 moves north to the western portion of the forest; and State Highway 169 intersects with U.S. Route 53 at Virginia and continues north to Ely in the center of the forest.

For more information: The Laurentian Divide is a ridge of low hills in northern Minnesota's Superior National Forest, separating the headwaters of streams that flow north and south. The crest between Tanner and Divide Lakes marks the divide. Waters to the north of here flow to the Arctic Ocean through Tanner Lake and the Dumbbell, Kawishiwi, Rainy, and Nelson Rivers. To the south the water bubbles toward the general direction of the Atlantic Ocean via Divide Lake, the Manitou River, the Great Lakes, and the St. Lawrence Seaway. For more details contact the Forest Supervisor, Superior National Forest, 8901 Grand Avenue Place, Duluth, MN 55801. Call 218-626-4300. The Voyageur Visitor Center east of Ely on State Highway 169 is a good place to get on-the-spot details. The center is open daily from May 1 through September 30.

Pets: Leashed.

Best time to visit: Year-round.

Activities: Hiking, mountain biking, snowmobiling, four-by-four driving, fishing, hunting, cross-country skiing, colorama tours.

Tettegouche State Park

One of the more recent additions to the state park system along U.S. Route 61, Tettegouche was established in 1979 and is still undergoing development of public facilities. As such, it remains rough and ready and a great fit for the rugged countryside. The 4,650 acres of parkland consist of mountains, a mile of Lake Superior shoreline, four inland lakes, rivers, waterfalls, and mile after mile of hardwood forests.

The best way to experience the park is by walking. Start at the Baptism River rest area along U.S. Route 61, where a footpath clambers up and over the lake bluff. You'll move through heavy groves of aspen and birch, whose silver leaves shimmer with each breeze. Soon you will move through cedar and black-ash country that had been completely logged over in the 1890s by the Alger-Smith Lumber Company. Thousands of rotting stumps, the only reminders of the virgin white-pine forests, roll away through the second-growth timber. The trail continues through white-spruce stands, which are today's major mature tree systems. Next (be prepared for heavy breathing) you begin to climb upward to the ridges overlooking Nipisiquit and Mic Mac Lakes. Keep your eyes open for the solitary white pine spared from the loggers' axes.

The Baptism River, which tumbles down from the Finland State Forest behind the park, has numerous photogenic waterfalls. Ingram Falls can only be spotted through the trees while driving northwest toward Ely on State Highway 1 from U.S. Route 61. However High Falls, Two Steps Falls, and The

Cascades can be viewed only from the hiking trail leading up from the highway rest stop and park entrance. A drive-in campground is located adjacent to Two Steps Falls, on the south side of the rampaging river. High Falls, which plummets with a roaring 80 feet of water over a ledge into a pool, is Minnesota's highest waterfall. It is a mile hike from the parking lot at the highway to the falls. A suspension bridge above the falls is part of the Superior Hiking Trail, which angles across the park. Seventeen miles of hiking trails with many scenic overlooks make the Tettegouche something special. Even the loggers from New Brunswick, who chopped their way up and down the slopes a century ago, were awestruck by the beauty. You can see the remains of one of their camps on the west shore of Mic Mac Lake, reached by a service road from County Highway 4, which you pick up in Beaver Bay, a mile south of Silver Bay. The Canadian lumbermen named the lake after one of the Algonquin tribes in their home province. Among the top trails in the park is the one that leads to the top of Mount Baldy, 1,000 feet above Lake Superior. If you squint (or carry binoculars), you can spot the dim forms of Wisconsin's Apostle Islands around the far southern rim of the lake. Another fine trek is the self-guided trail along the cliffs of Shovel Point, which also overlooks Lake Superior. Shovel Point, just northeast of the Baptism River, is an example of an ancient lava flow. This formation makes up part of the Sawtooth Mountains, which slope inland some 18 miles from Lake Superior. Get maps for the trail system that traverses the Sawtooths in the park information center.

Skiers love the 15 miles of groomed trail that are earmarked for intermediate and expert skiers. No bunny slopers here, folks, due to the steep drops and sharp turns. Snowshoers can also stretch their legs on designated trails inland to the lakes for ice fishing. Rugged individualists can also winter camp in the park, braving the mucho-minus temperatures and deep snow. Or bring a friend for snuggle time.

The park office, which is open year-round, has environmental and historical displays, with a great vista overlooking the surging waters of Lake Superior. Rangers there have regular interpretive programs discussing the flora and fauna of the region.

Where: The park is located in Lake County, four and a half miles northeast of Silver Bay on U.S. Route 61. Access to the park is from the Baptism River rest area.

For more information: Tettegouche State Park Manager, 5702 Highway 61 East, Silver Bay, MN 55614. Call 218-226-6365.

Amenities: There are 34 semimodern campsites and a heated sanitation building with flush toilets and showers. Two picnic areas, one at the Baptism River and the other at Nipisiquit Lake, offer excellent views of the lake and woods. As a reminder, only rowboats, kayaks, and canoes are allowed on the inland lakes. The craft must also be removed from the water each evening.

Pets: Keep them leashed and tied up.

Best time to visit: All year.

Activities: Rock climbing, fishing, hiking, camping, scenic overviews, picnicking. Snowmobilers can unload in the wayside rest parking lot and follow the markers to the Finland, Silver Bay, and North Shore Trails.

3

Central

Minnesotans who live in the heart of their state are truly lucky. They have the glitz and razzmatazz of the Twin Cities, with their professional ball teams, galleries, bars, restaurants, and extended parklands running through Hennepin, Ramsey, and contiguous counties. But it is only minutes in any direction for more remote and not-so-remote adventures, whether the traveler is a confirmed central-city dweller or 'burbanite. Timber, lakes, and prairies are at the cities' collective doorsteps. Snowmobiling, hiking, canoeing, horseback riding, backcountry driving, photography, birdwatching. Whew! The list of activities is seemingly endless . . . and all within what seems to be only a short sneeze from the cushioned front row of marvelous Tyrone Guthrie Theater or paper-laden legislative offices hunkered under the state capitol's impressive dome. Pine, Carlton, Aitkin, and the other counties banding central Minnesota have been rescued from the previous century's general disregard for the beauty of the land. A few white pines and prairie lands, reminders of earlier days, remain as proud survivors. The trees with six-foot-diameter trunks and towering arms dwarf their second-growth oak and maple neighbors throughout the St. Croix delta and similar watersheds draining the region into the Mississippi.

Among popular getaways within a two-hour driving distance from Minneapolis–St. Paul are the Chengwatana State

Forest with its Snake River Campground and Redhorse Hiking and Ski Touring Trail; Birch Lakes State Forest and the Tamarack River Equestrian Camp within the St. Croix State Forest; and the Land O'Lakes State Forest, about 140 miles west of Duluth and 188 miles north of Minneapolis–St. Paul. The 24-mile-long Ben Draper snowmobile trail, seven miles north of Outing on State Highway 6 in LOL State Forest, has been rated one of the tops in the state by die-hard sled fans because of its scenic variety. I would certainly be remiss if I didn't mention Banning Rapids on the Kettle River, four miles north of Pine County's city of Sandstone, where kayaking and canoeing are as challenging as anywhere in the North Country. Two miles of rough-and-tough water are tagged with such picturesque handles as Blueberry Slide, Mother's Delight, Dragon's Tooth, Little Banning, and Hell's Gate—any one of which can turn hair white as you bob and grunt through its rapids. Wise, experienced—and gutsy—water hounds don helmets and life jackets for their runs. But, oh, what fun. In fact the Minnesota Canoe Association holds its annual spring and fall jaunts through the gorge. However . . . Warning . . . Warning . . . Warning. These rapids are not kid's stuff, an amusement park ride with an extra thrill. A number of inexperienced kayakers have lost their lives here over the years, because they ignored the real danger and took chances without the proper gear.

On the calmer side, but just as wild when it comes to nature, are the 7,000 acres of the Wild River State Park, 14 miles east of I-35 just off State Highway 95 and County Highway 12. The park is one of the five largest in Minnesota, offering 35 miles of hiking trails along the federally designated "wild river," the St. Croix. Of all the state parks, this is one of the best for getting up close, real close, to wildlife. For instance, the park's Sunrise Trail is minimally maintained as it meanders through delightfully diverse habitats. This allows the visitor to walk up almost unnoticed (or so we like to think) on woodchucks, foxes, beavers, otters, and all sorts of birds. There's hardly a bigger thrill than seeing a marsh hawk plunge out of the sky, talons ready for its pick-up-and-go lunch. Savanna Portage State Park offers the hiker and fishing fan 15,000 acres of woods and lakes to explore, only 17,000 miles northeast of McGregor. Listen closely. You may hear the distant ghost song of long-dead French voyageurs as they make their spirit way through the bogs and swamps on the East Savanna River portage. This was once a major link between the Mississippi and St. Louis Rivers for traders and trappers. I'll bet you'll pick up the tune on a moonstruck night somewhere behind the primitive group camp on Savanna Lake. If not, you aren't listening hard enough.

Charles A. Lindbergh State Park

I've always wondered if Charles A. (Lucky Lindy) Lindbergh picked up his love of flying by watching the bald eagles soaring high above his home in Little Falls. He may have lain on his back along the banks of Pike Creek near where it enters the thick, muddy waters of the Mississippi River, watching those magnificent birds perform their aerial poetry. If my imagination is correct, Lindbergh the kid was already flying in his mind, arms outstretched and mind racing ahead of his time to Lindbergh the adult. Of course years later, he became the first pilot to make a solo flight to Europe and earned a second nickname as the Lone Eagle. The Lindbergh park was established in 1931, when 110 acres were donated to the state in memory of the famed aviator's dad, Charles A. Lindbergh Sr. In the 1960s, more land was added, increasing its size to 328 wooded acres.

Young Lindy lived in a one-and-a-half-story house, built by his father in 1906, on the current park grounds and managed his father's farm there for two years before leaving for college in 1920. Lindbergh Sr. was a respected progressive Republican congressman who represented central Minnesota in Washington from 1907 to 1917. He ran for governor in 1918 but was defeated, going on to be a leader in the Nonpartisan League. That political power block was the forerunner of today's Farmer Labor Party in Minnesota.

The house on the grounds is packed with Lindbergh memorabilia from several generations of the family. The 1916 Saxon auto used by Charles Sr. on his gubernatorial campaign is parked there. The Minnesota Historical Society administers the homesite and an informative interpretive center. The home is open daily during the summer. The center building is open on weekends throughout the winter.

The Lindberghs were not the first family to live alongside the rolling creek at the juncture of the Mississippi. Artifacts and burial mounds from the Woodland Culture, dating from 1000 B.C. to A.D. 1700 have been found throughout the woods. The Mississippi, of course, also served as a main watery highway for the Dakota who regularly camped in the region. The Red River Oxcart Trail also passed near the park on the east side of the Father of Waters. That segment was known as the Woods Trail, which reached from Pembina, North Dakota, back toward St. Paul. Southeast of the park is the user-friendly Charles A. Weyerhauser Museum, operated by the Morrison County Historical Society. The free museum is open year-round and has Native American artifacts and displays on early settlers.

The stands of oak throughout the park, along with patches of prairie, are similar to what was the landscape prior to Anglo arrival. On the south side of the park are stands of jack, white, and Norway pine, while the more grassy areas are on the north. Geologists explain that the land was molded by glacial action from 100,000 to 10,000 years ago, forming a "till plain." This broad, flat area is made up of gravel, clay, and other debris dumped by the glaciers. You can see some boulders left behind by the melting ice in the Pike Creek streambed. The rocks are under a trail bridge just to the west of the park's main parking lot, near where some ancient slate was also formed by what amounted to the earth's bowel movements. Mallards, black ducks, Canada geese, and other waterfowl regularly use the Mississippi River Flyway on their spring and autumn migrations. Lindy would have seen the forerunners of these birds, plus the great-great-grandparents of the deer, raccoons, owls, and other critters who now live in the fields and forests around what was his homestead.

While not as remote or as large as some of Minnesota's state parks, Lindbergh offers a quiet getaway, a touch of history, a brush with a famous personality, and plenty of opportunity for hiking or cross-country skiing. What is best, Lindbergh park is only minutes from downtown Little Falls, a quiet Minnesota community that is rich in history because of its location. Subsequently, you get the best of several worlds when coming through town and by stopping at the park for a visit. Eons ago the Mississippi's muscle cut a waterfall through some of that same slate formation that you find in the park itself. Hence the town's name.

Where: The park can be found in central Morrison County, two miles south of Little Falls. The entrance is off Lindbergh Drive (County Highway 52).
For more information: Charles A. Lindbergh State Park Manager, Box 364, Little Falls, MN 56345.
Call 320-616-2525.
Hours: The aviator's home is open from 10:00 A.M. to 5:00 P.M., Monday through Saturday, and from noon to 5:00 P.M., Sunday, May 1 to Labor Day; 10:00 A.M. to 4:00 P.M., Saturday, and noon to 4:00 P.M.,

Sunday, Labor Day to late October. The home is open other times to groups with prior reservations.

Admission: $6.50 for adults, with discounts for seniors, children, and groups. If you join the Minnesota Historical Society, you can receive free admission to any of the state's historic sites including the Lindbergh home.

Amenities: There are 38 semimodern campsites, one canoe camping area, a group camp for 50 persons, showers, trailer dump station, and a picnic area with an enclosed shelter. Six miles of hiking and skiing trails wend through the woods and across the prairie within the park. A public boat ramp is located on the Mississippi River. Take advantage of the scenic overlooks on the west side of the creek. They are easily reached via the trails.

Pets: Leashed.

Best time to visit: Year-round.

Activities: Camping, hiking, cross-country skiing, historical observation, fishing.

Crow Wing State Park

This park has an eclectic blend of Native American and pioneer history, wilderness, and river and recreational opportunities. Located where the Crow and the Mississippi Rivers marry, the site has long been inhabited. Curly Head (*Be be sig aun dib way*), Hole in the Day (*Bug o na ge shig*), and Strong Ground (*Song uk um eg*) were three well-known tribal leaders in the days when white-pine forests covered the landscape. The Indians called the river *Ka-gi-wig-wan* or "Raven's Wing." French explorers later dubbed it *Rivier Aile de Corbeau*, or "River of the Wing of the Raven." Subsequent generations boiled all that down to simply "Crow Wing."

The park lies within Cass, Crow Wing, and Morrison Counties. It lay on the route of the great oxcart trains that rumbled out of the Twin Cities to provision outposts and towns in the far reaches of Minnesota and the Dakotas. The squeaking wooden wheels of the carts could be heard for miles as they trundled along at two miles per hour on the Red River Trail, the superhighway of that era. The town of Crow Wing grew to be a major trading post and refurbishment center for the wagon trains as they headed west. Even after the advent of the steamboats, which put the overland transport companies out of business, Crow Wing remained a viable economic center at the edge of what passed for civilization in that era. Catholic, Episcopalian, and Lutheran clergy battled uphill for the souls in the frontier community, a village known more for its saloons than for attendance at St. Francis of Xavier Church, the Church of the Holy Cross, or the Lutheran Mission. If it wasn't the oxcart drivers, whose salty tongues could peel the hide of their castrated bulls (which is an apt Websterisque definition of the plodding ox), it was the lumber crews who used Crow Wing for rest and rehabilitation after a season in the woods. All in all, it was a rowdy bunch who lived there.

All this came to a screeching halt in the late 1860s when the Northern Pacific Railroad crossed the Mississippi River at Brainerd, rather than Crow Wing. Within a few years nothing was left of the town but some building foundations, as the home folks packed up and left for better economic opportunities along the rail line. Today you can poke around the few remains and look at the historic-site marker adjacent to the interpretive center. There are also deep tracks left by the huge oxcarts along the shore of the river. The spirits of Father Francis X. Pierz, the Reverend E. Steele Peake, and the Reverend Ottmar Cloetter will be there all right, just as will those of Allen Morrison, C. H. Beaulieu, H. M. Rice, and other early village residents. Standing near the picnic tables on the bluffs overlooking the Mississippi, it is easy to hear the chants of the Dakota, the crack of the teamsters' rawhide whips, and the rumble of the wagon trains. Or is that just the wind?

Across the river is the Camp Ripley Military Reservation, although you won't see much army activity amid the thick aspen and oak over there. The original Fort Ripley was estab-lished in 1848 to keep an eye on the bands of Sioux and Ojib-way still roaming the region through the 1860s. Today the troopers stick to themselves in their barracks and bivouacs, but a military plane occasionally swoops along the river like a frantic bat. When that happens, keep hiking or skiing and ignore the modern intrusion.

To the north of the park, the Crow Wing River begins in a series of Hubbard County lakes formed by the melting of buried glacial ice. Each lake is numbered from one to 11, with the latter being considered the headwater of the river. The lakes cover an estimated 5,000 acres, with the connecting river flowing 100 miles through heavy stands of pine, oak, and maple to its eventual merger with the Mississippi at Old Crow Wing, site of the state park. Fishing fans love the various lakes, each with its principal species, depending on depth. The upper lakes are better for panfish and bass, while the lower ones feature pike and walleye. Numerous smaller rivers and streams flow into the Crow on its trip southward. Most can be canoed. Bring suntan lotion, cushions, pole and bait, mosquito repellent, fruit juice, and maybe a good Dutch Masters cigar. Ah, for the life on the river.

Where: The park is nine miles south of Brainerd on State Highway 371, with its headquarters on County Highway 27, one mile off 371. The highway is part of the federally desig-nated Great River Road, which runs the length of the Mis-sissippi. Little Falls is 19 miles to the southwest.

For more information: Crow Wing State Park, 7100 State Park Road SW, Brainerd, MN 56401. Call 218-829-8022.

Amenities: Crow Wing State Park has 61 semimodern camp-sites and one primitive group camp along the east bank of the winding Mississippi River. There is also one canoe campsite able to accommodate 50 persons, with hand water pumps and toilets. The watercraft camping area is about a half mile north of the group camp. For those who appreciate their more mod-ern conveniences, a trailer dump station is located in the park, and there are 12 sites with electricity. The park features an enclosed picnic shelter for those rainy, windblown days that tend to sneak up on Minnesota outdoors folks at the least opportune time—such as weekends, holidays, and any other days off.

Fifty tables are scattered around two other spacious out-door picnic areas. Ice and wood are sold in the camping area by park staff. Hands off downed wood, and heaven help any-one chopping a live tree. For those of you seeking exercise, there are 14 miles of footpaths to explore, a four-mile self-guided interpretive trail, 6.4 miles of cross-country ski trails, and 11½ miles of snowmobile trails. As with all state parks, a daily or annual permit is required for entering. The permit can be purchased at the park headquarters.
Pets: Leashed and tethered or don't bring.
Best time to visit: Year-round.
Activities: Camping, interpretive programs, fishing, hiking, cross-country skiing, canoeing.

Father Hennepin State Park

There had to be a park named after the spiritual explorer of the Minnesota wilderness. Black-robed Father Louis Hen-nepin, a Jesuit on the quest for souls, was one of the first recorded European adventurers to visit what is now Min-nesota. Actually historians don't call it a "visit" in the sense that the young Belgian and two French voyageur companions were on holiday. They were actually captives, seized by the Dakota Sioux in 1679 while exploring the St. Anthony Falls area where Minneapolis now stands. The Native Americans didn't know quite what to do with the trio so they were brought to the area of Mille Lacs Lake in 1679 and held prisoner. Sieur Duluth rescued them in 1681, trekking through the forest from his fortified trading post/encampment at Grand Portage on Lake Superior. Hennepin's captivity did not deter the good priest from continuing to poke around Minnesota for a short time before returning to Europe. He died in 1701 in Rome.

The park itself, located in Mille Lacs County on the southeast shore of Mille Lacs Lake, is not the actual site where Hennepin and his partners were held, although the Indian camp was probably in the vicinity. Covering 316 acres, the park was created in 1941, making it one of the most mature in the state. It is tucked into a headland formed in the west side of Isle Bay on Mille Lacs, the second largest body of fresh water within Minnesota. During Hennepin's day the region was densely forested with cloud-shredding white pine along the rivers and dotted with marshes. Today, years after the loggers had done their work in the last century, the landscape is carpeted with second-growth oaks and maples. Aspen stands are full of grouse, which explode from the undergrowth in heart-stopping flutters. Only a few of the pines remain as a testimonial to the Native Americans and explorers who made first contact with them.

Bird life is a major draw for outdoor lovers. Eagles, ospreys, and a variety of hawks are regularly seen winging overhead. Beaver, deer, mink, and raccoon are plentiful. Keep an eye on the ground for their tracks.

Where: The park is located one mile west of Isle, off State Highway 27.

For more information: Father Hennepin State Park Manager, Box 397, Isle, MN 56342. Call 612-676-8763.

Amenities: One of the better scenic views is along the lakeshore between the two docks and boat launches, north of the campground closest to the water. Standing there on a cool autumn evening, you can put yourself in Hennepin's worn brogans, wondering if rescue would ever come and whether or not the tribes would listen to his message of salvation. Father Hennepin State Park has 103 semimodern campsites with water, toilets, and showers; 30 of the sites have electricity. Hennepin should have been so lucky. A trailer dump station is located near the parking lot beyond the information center. Two picnic shelters augment the picnic tables scattered throughout the park grounds. Four miles of hiking trails let today's adventurers explore the lakeshore and surrounding forests.

Foothills State Forest/ Spider Lake Ski Trail

Loggers went through this region of central Minnesota as if they were possessed. Hardly a stick with a diameter wider than three inches was left standing by the early 1900s. Saws and axes leveled thousands of acres of white pine, leaving the ground exposed to the erosive elements. Next came the hard-scrabble homesteaders who dreamed of fertile fields, rich crops, and economic security. They got nothing. The land, battered and abandoned by the timber companies, was too rocky for agriculture. The thin topsoil, a perfect ecosystem for timber growth, was not suitable for corn and wheat.

The railroads that served the logging camps shut down, further isolating the few farmers who hung on by a thin thread of equity and barrels of sweat. Eventually they too followed the tracks and departed. By the 1930s few people lived in the vicinity amid the rundown remains of long-gone neighbors' homes and barns. Second growth began healing the scars of logging roads and clear-cut chopping. The state stepped in in 1931 to establish the Foothills State Forest in an effort to revitalize the rolling landscape, protect the watershed, and take care of the remaining natural resources. Today 43,960 acres are within the forest boundaries. The Minnesota Division of Forestry administers 17,900 acres and Cass County manages 12,500 acres. The remainder is in private hands. Hundreds of glacial lakes and potholes dot the ground, sparkling like fat diamonds when seen from the air.

Today a visitor can see contemporary logging practices at work as the state allows up to 3,000 cords of wood to be harvested annually on public lands within the forest. The cuttings are replanted, unlike after the previous century's butchery. Two lookout towers are irregularly staffed during the summer months as a fire-prevention service. Insect pests are monitored by state Forest Service workers and careful observation of the wildlife keeps the Foothills State Forest a veritable natural zoo. Deer, porcupines, skunks, hawks, and hundreds of other species call the place their home. Speak softly, walk quietly, and you'll see plenty of animal action.

Among the many recreation possibilities within the forest are the Foothills Snowmobile Trail (which connects with the Chippewa, Cass County Snoway, Heartland, and Aspen snowmobile routes), the Spider Lake ski trail, and the Cut Lake Ski Trail.

Spider Lake Trail is a 13-mile groomed pathway that both beginners and advanced skiers can appreciate. To get to the trailhead from Pine River, take County Highway 2 for 10 miles west and watch for the signage. The Cut Lake Trail is an 11-mile groomed trail just to the north of the Spider Lake circuit. Two south loops on the Spider Lake leg are not groomed, however, which adds to the enjoyment, especially with newly fallen snow. So get out early before the rest of the area's snow fans rise and take advantage of the powder. There are several difficult sections along Spider Lake Trail, two of which are in the vicinity of the fire watchtower. Steep slopes and quick turns are great tests of your braking and banking abilities. More surprised folks tumble here than you would expect, whipping around a bend atop a crest and finding themselves immediately diving down into a pothole valley. The descents can be gulpers. But don't discount the fantastic fun.

Where: The Foothills State Forest is located in central Cass County, 40 miles northwest of Brainerd. The sprawl of timberland is west of State Highway 371 and the communities of Pine River, Backus, and Hackensack. For easy access State Highway 64 runs through the southwestern section of the woods.

For more information: Backus Area Forest Supervisor, Box 6, Backus, MN 56435. Call 218-947-3232; or DNR Regional Headquarters, 1601 Minnesota Drive, Brainerd, MN 56401. Call 218-828-2561.

Pets: Leashed.

Best time to visit: Anytime, but winter skiing is high on the list of seasonal fun.

Activities: Boating, picnicking, ski touring.

Other: There are numerous canoe- and boating-access ramps within the Foothills State Forest. Bass, crappies, lake trout, muskies, and walleyes abound in Hand, Woman, Widow, Island, Mow, and Norway Lakes. Public water access maps, easily secured from the Minnesota Department of Natural Resources show you where these are. Ask for the Upper Cass Wadena, and Lower Cass Counties selections. Most have concrete drives into the water; however, even the dirt ramps are easy in and easy out.

Mille Lacs Kathio State Park and Rum River State Forest

Located only 80 miles north of the Twin Cities, the 10,000-acre Mille Lacs Kathio State Park is the fourth largest state park in Minnesota. The region has had 4,000 years of human habitation, with the Native Americans finding the natural abundance of game and the fertile soil perfect for supplying food to their settlements. The wild rice along Ogechie Lake, a long shallow lake near today's park campground, was long a staple of tribal diets. It still is a veritable natural foods outpost for the Indian nation's members who continue to live nearby. But even before the Dakota and Ojibway, a pre-Indian people who fashioned tools from copper had a village where a park picnic area is now located. *Kathio* is a translation of the Dakota word *Isatys*, meaning "those who pitched tents at the Knife Lake." Subsequently there is an overwhelming sense of history in Mille Lacs Kathio. You feel its presence while putting your canoe into the Rum River (a mistranslation of the Native American word for "Spirit River," early settlers thinking the word referred to alcoholic spirits). This feeling about the past is also ever present when you're cross-country skiing down the tricky slopes on the north side of Black Bass Lake. And it is there at the interpretive center, which is adjacent to the Indian tribal lands on the east side of Ogechie Lake, near the swimming beach. The facility tells the story of the tribes, who put their marks on the land, as well as outlining the tale of white development and resulting environmental concerns.

The landscape within the park is considered a terminal moraine, formed by a retreating glacier only 10,000 years ago. As the glacier melted, it dumped millions of tons of rocks and boulders that it had scooped up on its grinding passage over northern Minnesota. These deposits are known as *moraines*. All this natural junk formed a dam that blocked the rivers that ran through here, forming a lake even larger than the current Mille Lacs Lake, which is on the eastern side of the state park.

Over the generations, new drainage routes reshaped the land. Today's park is the result of wave and ice action on the lake, the silting of ponds, and outlet streams cutting new channels. As the land changed, so did the people who lived here. In the late 1600s French explorer Daniel Greysolon, Sieur Duluth (after whom the city of Duluth is named), came through the area, as did Father Louis Hennepin. In the 1700s most of the Dakota moved on as the buffalo herds moved farther west. After a bloody three-day battle in 1745 at Kathio between a cluster of Dakota villages along the Rum River and the Ojibway, the Ojibway won and brought their own traditions and culture from the east. Other rounds of warfare between roaming bands of both nations occurred as late as 1839. In one ambush Dakota warriors killed some 70 Ojibway, mostly women and children, in revenge for the murder of one of their people. In the 1850s the area was heavily logged for its white and red pine. Subsequently, the contemporary state park is full of aspen, birch, maple, and oak. You can get a fine feel for this area by climbing to the top of the 100-foot-high observation tower in the center of the park, reached by following the main park road beyond the information center. Dress for the weather. Once atop the tower on chilly days, it is a long way back down for a sweater. Fog can also roll inland unexpectedly, building up like a great cotton ball as it edges up from the lake to limit your sight line to the hand at the end of your arm. That can be disconcerting on the tower, knowing there is nothing between you and the ground but gunpowder-colored vapor wisps.

Mille Lacs Lake is the headwater of the canoe-perfect Rum River, which flows through the Rum River State Forest. The woodland is made up mostly of tax-forfeited old farmsites, now consisting of 33,180 acres of maple, oak, ash, basswood on the uplands, and ash and elm around the swampy areas. There are scattered stands of tamarack. The Rum eventually makes its way 140 miles to the Mississippi River. En route it hits Ogechie and Shakopee lakes and Lake Onamia. When it begins its journey, the shallow waters are extremely clear, but the river muddies out as it travels along. Tributaries have a tendency to deposit silt as they join the river on its trip. While canoeing watch out for snags along the stretch between Princeton and Cambridge—gooey marshland along the banks here makes foot travel nigh impossible. The mud flats have a distinctive, rotting vegetable odor on hot August days, but that probably never bothers the raccoons and other creatures who scurry down the banks for a drink in the evening. Their paw prints are abstracts across the drying crust, giving testimony to the teeming lifestyles along the river. Dense stands of hardwoods are inland, muffling the sounds of traffic along state and county roadways. A 35-mile stretch of the river, between Cambridge and Anoka, is not as isolated—there are many manicured lawns running to the river's edge as you approach the Twin Cities. The river broadens out and moves faster as it approaches the Mississippi. The smooth flowage and lack of rough riding make the Rum fine for beginner and intermediate paddlers. But according to veteran boaters, in low water you may have to portage near the Milaca Dam or pull your canoe over the gravel below St. Francis.

Put in just about anywhere along the river: at the Mille Lacs Kathio State Park or at waysides at Milaca, Princeton,

Cambridge, Isanti, and St. Francis. You can even launch a canoe from the county park behind the fairgrounds in Anoka. Canoe rentals and a shuttle service are available during the summer. Bring a fishing pole, lures, and bait for the monster bass and pike that are just waiting for you out there amid the rocks and riffles. The overhanging trees make great shade for such wily fish. Good luck.

Within the Rum River State Forest, the 14-mile-long Hoot Owl Trail in Mille Lacs County is groomed and signed for winter snowmobilers. Hikers and horseback riders can take advantage of the system in the other seasons. To get to the trailhead, take U.S. Route 169 north for 14 miles from Milaca. Then turn right (east) on Mille Lacs County Highway 20 and drive four miles. The 5.3-mile-long Kanabec Trail in Kanabec County is also a great snowmobilers' route, to be enjoyed by hikers and riders in the spring, summer, and autumn. This trail can be entered along Kanabec County Highways 10, 26, 55, and 56. Look for the signs pointing the way to the park. A cool, comfortable little picnic area on the forest road off Kanabec County Highway 56 is a real treasure. It is marked and easy to find. There is a 1½-mile nature trail there as well, perfect for youngsters just discovering the wonders of the wilderness.

Where: The main park entrance is one mile off U.S. Route 169 on County Highway 26. The Rum River State Forest is between western Kanabec and northern Mille Lacs Counties. Most of the forest is between State Highway 47 and U.S. Route 169 south of the Mille Lacs Wildlife Management Area. Another part of the state forest is reached via Mille Lacs County Highway 20 east from U.S. Route 169. Drive two miles and you are there at the gate.
For more information: Mille Lacs Kathio State Park Manager, 15066 Kathio State Park Road, Onamia, MN 56359. Call 612-532-3523; DNR Area Forest Supervisor, 915 South County

Highway 65, Cambridge, MN 55008. Call 612-689-2832; DNR Area Forest Supervisor, Route 2, 701 South Kenwood Street, Moose Lake, MN 55767. Call 218-485-4474.

Hours: The state park is open throughout the year, with gates down from 10:00 P.M. to 8:00 A.M., except for registered campers.

Pets: Leashed and tied. Keep them out of park buildings and historic sites.

Best time to visit: Year-round.

Activities: Camping, fishing, bird-watching, exploring historic areas.

Other: Keep the firearms, explosives, air guns, slingshots, traps, seines, nets, bows and arrows, and all other weapons at home.

Moose Lake Recreational Area

I have yet to see a moose at Moose Lake, but that doesn't mean that someday I won't be lucky and spy one of Minnesota's semiofficial mascots. The recreation area was established in 1971, pulling together 965 acres, with easy access from I-35. A sandy beach along Echo Lake on the park's southern side and hiking/cross-country ski trails make the Moose Lake area a popular getaway for residents of Duluth, the closest city. Moosehead Lake is on the northeast side of the park. I would suggest reservations for any of the 18 rustic campsites at Moose Lake. They are snatched up fast, especially during peak summer weekends in July and August and during the autumn colorama. There are picnic grounds in the park.

Where: Moose Lake Recreational Area is in Carlton County, one mile east of I-35 at the Moose Lake exit. The park gate is off County Highway 137.

For more information: Moose Lake Recreation Area Manager, 1000 County Highway 137, Route 2, Moose Lake, MN 55767. Call 218-245-3382.
Pets: Leashed.
Best time to visit: Summer (for swimming).
Activities: Fishing, swimming, hiking, snowmobiling, skiing.

Otter Tail County

When Minnesotans talk water, they talk Otter Tail County, literally the Land of a Thousand Lakes. In the heart of the resort-dotted county, the rolling waters of Otter Tail Lake comprise 13,725 acres. One of the largest counties in the state, Otter Tail has some of the best fishing, hiking, skiing, and other outdoor recreation opportunities in the Midwest. Maplewood State Park, seven miles southeast of Pelican Rapids on State Highway 108, is a hilly leap above the surrounding farmlands. Established in 1963, the park and its 9,000 acres showcase one of the best stands of hardwoods in west-central Minnesota. As such it is popular for autumn color tours and just-before-winter camping at its 66 sites. A rentable A-frame house, surrounded by the forest, overlooks Wilson Pond. The heated DNR-managed property sleeps 14, featuring two bathrooms and a pan-cutlery-crockery-supplied kitchen, as well as a garage. Bring your own linens and towels. Rentals are available through the state park reservation network. The best scenery is seen from the hills above Lake Lida, formed by glaciers 20,000 years ago. There is an extensive horseback-riding system throughout the entire park, which complements the cross-country, snowmobile, and hiking trails.

   Tim Bodeen of the U.S. Fish and Wildlife Service is manager of the Prairie Wetlands Learning Center. The site is just south of Fergus Falls, adjacent to the West Otter Tail County Fairgrounds.

Bodeen is excited about the potential of the 300-acre center, which opened in 1993, and he talks animatedly of it as monarch butterflies flutter around the prairie flowers, such as sunflowers and big bluestem. The colorful insects flock in orange and black swirls across the center's slopes, hills that have never felt a steel plow. A 200-year-old oak, nicknamed Alice by visiting school kids, is the grandma tree in a savanna near one of the 27 wetlands on the property. The variety of landscape in such proximity to a major Minnesota city is an educational boon. He hosts seasonal seminars, flower-planting sessions, and guided trail experiences. In the summer Bodeen even reads aloud to youngsters from Laura Ingalls Wilder's *Little House on the Prairie.* He sits them down amid the tall grasses so they get a feel for the earth, much as Laura, her sister Mary, and their family did.

The Fergus Falls Fish and Game Club and other community groups were instrumental in pushing for establishment of the learning center, Bodeen pointed out. Mushrooming local and state support for environmental education, as well as realization that migratory waterfowl needed protection, led to the site's establishment.

An outdoor amphitheater near an old barn, the last vestige of a farm there, was made by Eagle Scout Joel Harris and other members of Troop 302. They were aided by area contractors. The oak-shaded seats are perfect for orientation, especially on a breezy summer afternoon. Sitting there it is easy to imagine buffalo grazing around the prairie onion and wild sage on the nearby slopes.

The Seven Sisters are seven small knobs in a hilly section of the prairie on the north side of Lake Christina. A 148-acre nature conservancy site in this area showcases a sedge meadow and other marsh vegetation typical of the glacial-pothole country. The hikable Sisters are located three miles northeast of the town of Ashby on State Highway 78. You can't miss the knolls.

Great blue herons, egrets, and cormorants provide a bird-land song-and-dance show at Egret Island on Pelican Lake, just off Ashby. A warning: Stay off the 34-acre island from April to July, the nesting season. But you can canoe or motor up to the rocky spit any other time. A public boat access on the lake is on the east side of State Highway 78, two miles south of town, and about two miles north of Exit 77 on I-94. Forty species of birds have been recorded on the island, making it excellent for the binocular set.

Where: The county is accessible via U.S. Route 10 and I-94 from the Twin Cities (about a four-hour drive). Other major highways leading into the region include Highway 210 from the Dakotas in the west and U.S. Route 59 from southern Minnesota.

For more information: Otter Tail County Tourism Association, Box 1000, Ottertail, MN 56571; Maplewood State Park, Route 3, Box 422, Pelican Rapids, MN 56572. Call 218-863-8383; Friends of the Prairie Wetlands Learning Center, Box 23, Fergus Falls, MN 56537.

Pets: Sure, but keep 'em leashed.

Best time to visit: Year-round

Activities: Hunting, fishing, loafing, water skiing, hiking, skiing.

Other: As a resort community, there is plenty to do when kids tire of inner tubing and trekking. At 9:30 A.M. each Wednesday in summer, turtle races are held in the parking lot of Perham's Super Value food store. Kids—and an occasionally lucky adult, such as Bruce Asbury, weatherman/reporter for Fargo's KXJB-TV—stand in a ring, releasing their "steeds" when a starting whistle is blown. Winners of each heat receive a blue ribbon and a dollar prize, and other prizes are awarded to the final champ. Turtles are released back into the wild after Labor Day. Of course there's always more to do in resort country. Note the walleye tournament on West Battle Lake at the end of June and the Pelican Rapids Art in the Park show in late July. Hungry resort guests never miss the mid-August turkey barbecue in Henning. Nearby New York Mills, a former lumbering center where some folks on the street still speak Finnish, has several activities that should be on a vacationer's to-do list. The village hosts the Great American Think-Off each June, in which debaters from around the country discuss such topics as "Does society value money or morality?" New York Mills also holds the annual Finn Creek Folk Festival each August.

Paul Bunyan State Forest

It is only proper that Minnesota's honorary giant has a forest named in his honor. Paul Bunyan, that mythological logger, and his giant ox, Babe, have so long been a part of the state's folklore that some folks probably think the brawny, bearded guy is governor . . . or at least a state legislator. Among the feats credited to Bunyan brawn are digging Puget Sound, dredging the St. Lawrence River, and carving out the Grand Canyon. Needless to say, the old boy was pretty busy before he arrived in Minnesota. Some authorities, especially the good old boys around public radio's Sidetrack Tap at Lake Woebegon, say the Bunyan legend evolved from folktales retold in Quebec or northern Ontario. But a tried-and-true Minnesotan has just as much claim to the fable as any *Quebecois*. Bunyan's blue bovine buddy, Babe, was supposedly so big that the distance between his horns was variously described as 24 ax handles and a plug of tobacco to 42 ax handles. Statues of

Bunyan and Babe can be seen on the lakefront in Bemidji. They were erected in 1937, and their annual painting and sprucing up is the real harbinger of spring in Central Minnesota.

You won't find the giant logger or Babe in the Paul Bunyan State Forest; however the logging traditions are still alive. Aspen harvesting in the forest averages 31,500 cords of wood a year, with two wafer-board plants in Bemidji keeping up with the demand. Currently 82 percent of the forest is aspen, with 10 percent of it in pine and 8 percent in hardwoods, such as maple and oak. Unlike the old days when timber companies simply took and never replaced, more than five million seedlings have been planted in the state forest over the past three decades. About four million of the plantings are red

Paul Bunyan and Babe the Blue Ox

pine, with jack pine and white spruce making up much of the remainder.

The forest was not always so lucky. The Red River Lumber Company took a swing at the woods in the early 1900s and removed millions of board feet of timber within a few years. By 1911 a sawmill in the village of Akeley had a capacity of producing 500,000 square feet of lumber per day. Logs were hauled across Eleventh Crow Wing Lake to the mill where they were sliced, diced, and trimmed for delivery to urban centers in the south. In 1910 up to 5,000 men labored in the woods, working out of 10 camps. Railroads crisscrossed the forest, forming the base of several of today's forest roads, such as Spur 1 and the Gulch Lake Forest Trail.

In 1915 the Red River Lumber Company pulled out and moved to California. Small operators continued to log the region until the 1920s, when they too left after all the harvestable timber was gone. The population dropped 80 percent in the space of a few years when the cutters left. In 1935, after years of political wrangling, the state forest was established. A state game refuge is within the forest's southern unit, to the west of State Highway 64.

There are several great campgrounds within the forest, especially at Mantrap Lake and Gulch Lake. Mantrap is the larger of the two, with 38 campsites, a picnic area, swimming beach, and water access for boaters and fishermen. To find the camp area, take County Highway 4 (located between State Highways 200 and 34) to Emmaville. Then follow the signs on County Highway 24. A two-mile nature and ski-touring trail near Mantrap Lake is reached by driving past the campground on County Highway 104 to the East Mantrap Lake boat launch. Another trail for photography buffs, because of its beauty (especially in the autumn), is the Waboose Lake Trail between Spur 1 and the Akeley Cut-Off Forest Road.

Gulch Lake offers 10 sites in five units spread between Gulch, Nelson, and Bass Lakes and Lake Twenty-One. The West Gulch hiking trail connects to trails leading to the other campsites in the tiny system. These sites can be reached from the Halverson Forest Road east from County Highway 4 and on the Gulch Lake Forest Road west from State Highway 64.

Snowmobilers turn out in force in the frigid winter to experience the 50 miles of groomed trails and 15 miles of ungroomed ones meandering through Paul Bunyan. The trails traverse logging roads, some of which are plowed during the season. Be aware that as logging picks up around the first of each year, some of the roads are closed to snowmobilers because of the truck traffic. These routes can be used for hiking and horseback riding in the summer. But, again, watch out for traffic.

Where: The forest is tucked into the far reaches of Hubbard County, six miles north of Nevis and Akeley. You can get there via State Highway 34 from Walker or Park Rapids or by way of State Highway 64 from Laporte.

For more information: DNR Forestry Office, Box 113, 607 West First Street, Park Rapids, MN 56470. Call 218-732-3309; Minnesota DNR, Division of Forestry Information Center, 500 Lafayette Road, St. Paul, MN 55155-4040. Call 651-296-4484; Bemidji Area Forest Supervisor, 2220 Bemidji Avenue, Bemidji, MN 56601. Call 218-755-2890.

Pets: Leashed.

Best time to visit: Year-round.

Activities: Camping, hiking, horseback riding, boating, fishing, hunting, picnicking, swimming, cross-country skiing.

Other: You can hunt and fish in the forest as long as you have the proper license and follow state regulations. In addition both on-and off-trail hiking is permitted, as is the picking of fruit and mushrooms. The elusive—and delicious—morel can be found occasionally in early spring, another reason for enjoying a walk in the woods. Be sure you know what you're picking. Finding the rare mushroom within the 72,107 acres is part of the season's challenge. You can also pick up dead wood for campfires, but there is no cutting of fuel wood for home use on state land.

St. John's University

For quiet reflection, good bread, intellectual atmosphere, and excellent trails, St. John's University provides an interesting mix of wilderness and gentility. Since the university's founding in 1856 by German Benedictine monks, stewardship over its 2,400 acres has been paramount. It is now an official state wildlife refuge. Lumber harvesting, reforestation, water and soil management, contemporary waste treatment, and habitat restoration are old hat to the order's priests and brothers. The only noticeable European "intrusion" on what was once mostly prairie was an initial planting of pine groves more than a century ago. This was a curative for the homesickness of those early Bavarians who yearned for a memory of their beloved forests back home.

The plantation was the first in Minnesota, located behind what is now St. John's Preparatory School on the north side of Lake Sagatagan, one of seven lakes on the property. There are other groves located on the university campus, on a hill in the region called Pine Knob and along I-94, commonly known as the Pine Curtain. But another 1,500 acres of university property are forested with 24 species of hardwoods. Generations of the order's master craftsmen used the birch, maple, basswood, ash, and red and white oak to make furniture for the Benedictine Abbey on the grounds and for the school.

There are 12 miles of hiking and cross-country skiing trails through the wetlands, prairie, and forests at St. John's. A system map can be secured from the university's public relations office. The Stella Maris Chapel, on a rocky point across Lake Sagatagan from the main campus, is accessible via the trail. Standing above the beach at the school, you can see the ornate little building in its postcard setting. The beach, by the way, can be used only by students and faculty.

One link of the trail tiptoes through the "Sugar Bush" area of forest, where each spring some 1,500 maple taps are used to collect sap for syrup making.

Other notes: The university has restored 135 acres to their original condition, with another 50 acres of old farmland brought back to prairie since 1990. The section is bordered by I-94 and County Highway 159. A 60-acre wetland was regenerated in 1988. There is also a 25-acre oak savanna south of the wetlands. University spokespeople point out that their campus was once the transition landscape between the Big Woods on the east and the Great Plains on the west. They say controlled burning is still integral to maintaining the appropriate natural balance.

Oh what about the bread? St. John's deliciously wonderful wheat loaves are baked on-site and can be purchased at the school. The university invites any travelers along I-94 to drop by for lunch in the school cafeteria (no reservations necessary) or for a pit stop. Once on campus visitors admire the monumental abbey church, considered one of Minnesota's architectural landmarks. The Hill Monastic Manuscript Library on campus contains microfilm of thousands of illuminated documents dating back several centuries. In a twist linking the contemporary with the ancient, you can access the library via the Internet at www.csbsju.edu.

Where: The campus is 10 minutes west of St. Cloud, accessed off I-94. It is about 90 minutes west of the Twin Cities. Take the St. John's University exit from the freeway, turn left at the end of the ramp, where the road then leads to the campus center. Visitor parking is available in the central quadrangle.

For more information: St. John's University, Order of St. Benedict, Box 2015, Collegeville, MN 56321-2015. Call 320-363-2011.

Pets: No.

Best time to visit: All year.

Activities: Hiking, bird-watching, nature photography, skiing, educational pursuits.

Other: Self-guided or guided tours can be arranged at the visitors center in St. John's Sexton Commons.

4

Metro Area

Canoeing, trumpeter swans, bass fishing, white-tailed deer, hiking, butterflies—yep, all that within the Twin Cities metro area. Just because skyscrapers stab the blue Minnesota skies, barge traffic rolls down the Mississippi River, and one of the country's largest regional airports is part of the scenery, doesn't mean that you can't find blue false indigo or a wood duck. Thousands of acres have been set aside for the enjoyment and use of contemporary Twin Citians and for future generations. Despite the encroachment of strip malls, diminishing wetlands, and a host of turf-jealousies among cities and suburbs, any outdoors lover can still find plenty of getaway naturalness within a few blocks of home or hotel.

To protect open space in the urban area, the Minnesota legislature established a regional park network in 1974 that includes 29 regional parks, 10 larger park reserves, four trail corridors, and a floral display garden. These 45,000 acres are dotted through seven counties, offering a variety of big woods, moraine hills, river valleys, and prairies. Land is acquired with state money through the Metropolitan Council and advised by the Metropolitan Parks and Open Space Commission.

Six counties (Anoka, Carver, Hennepin, Ramsey, Washington, and Dakota), three cities (Minneapolis, St. Paul, and

Bloomington), and the Scott-Hennepin Park Advisory Board operate and maintain the parks within the regional system.

Hennepin Parks

In the early 1900s the Minneapolis Civic Commission advocated a park plan that included a broad belt of forest preserves around the city. Under the ensuing 30-year administration of park director Theodore Wirth, the plan was amended to include more recreational development. And as with most metro areas, green space within the community began disappearing at a rapid rate as population grew. There was concern that eventually all open land would be gone, so a metropolitan park system was established in the 1950s. It took several years of wrangling among cities and towns in Hennepin County, but compromises were worked out and the plan was implemented.

Today's mission statement of Hennepin Parks reads: "... to promote environmental stewardship through recreation and education in a natural resources–based park system."

The idea is clear: Take care of the land and you take care of the people.

The Hennepin system, which extends beyond Hennepin County to include Scott County, is charged with maintaining an intermediary recreation program with its accompanying facilities. While the state has its trails and wilderness campsites for a totally natural experience, and the city has organized sports programs, the Hennepin plan offers the middle ground, namely preserves and reserves within an urban mode.

"We are modeled after the hundred-year-old East Bay Regional Park District in California," said Tom McDowell, director of natural resources management for Hennepin

Parks. "We have subsequently identified large tracts of land to put some restraints on their development. We call it the 80-20 policy by which 80 percent of the parkland remains in its natural state, while 20 percent is set aside for informal playing fields, golf courses, picnic areas, and complementary recreation facilities," he explained.

With increasing urbanization there are still battles being waged in the county. "To me the big question is how well will we protect and defend the acreage set aside within our 80-20 plan," McDowell said. "Expectations remain that we will provide recreation opportunities to the entire population with creative play areas and the like, but we need to balance that with our need to preserve the natural beauty. Yet as the public demand grows, there is a broadening definition of what recreation is," he pointed out. Proponents of radio-controlled airplanes, hot-air balloons, motorized miniature boats, and in-line skating are all seeking space, said McDowell.

Since the communities do not want to remove any more land from the tax rolls, ideas for buffer strips around the existing parks have not gained much support in a more crowded environment. Municipalities "tell us to work within the land that we already have," McDowell indicated.

"Our legacy will not be in the recreational facilities we develop but in the protection of our undeveloped areas. I guess I am optimistic about it all. I tend to think there is a lot of the populace out there who believe in our mission," he said.

But he pointed out the problems with resource management in which the many layers of government mingle with builders' demands and the requirements of the public. "Decisions outside the parks impact the parks," he warned. "One city complains about loss of flood storage, yet at the same time it doesn't put any control on development," McDowell complained. However, he said, there is a growing realization that communities are seeing the parks as part of the solutions to their problems of urban runoff and related issues. "The agencies that make up the regional park system work well together . . . except when competing for the same dollars," he laughed.

McDowell has a degree in biology. This naturalist background makes him an enigma within the park management, most of whom have degrees in recreation or public administration. As a natural resources–based system, Hennepin Parks is committed to the ecological restoration of park reserve land, he emphasized. "In order to accomplish this goal, it is important that biological issues be considered in addition to the recreational needs of the park user," McDowell said.

"The real determinant as to whether we are successful with our mission is whether the public feels as strongly about protecting what we have as they do about development," he concluded.

In 1994 the park system celebrated the Year of Wildflowers, in an effort to raise public awareness of the important role the plants play in forests, prairies, and wetlands. Special programs relating to flowers were held at nature and visitors centers. There are also themes for other years.

There are many ways to see the parks and preserves. For bikers I suggest taking the North Trail Corridor, a 15-mile run that begins in Hopkins on the west side of Eighth Avenue, north of Main Street. It ends in Victoria near the intersection of Rose Lane and Stieger Road. The South Trail Corridor is an 11½-mile jaunt that starts in downtown Hopkins at the park-and-ride lot, southeast of the intersection of Eighth Avenue South and Excelsior Boulevard. The route concludes in central Chanhassen.

Canoeists can try a 10-mile run from Lake Rebecca to Crow-Hassan on the Crow River, which takes about three to four hours on some fast water. Most of the stream is lazy and relaxed. However, wear a life preserver. You can also paddle from Crow-Hassan to Dayton, a distance of some 16 miles, which takes about five hours. There is a bit of fast water and shallow rapids, as well as some interesting turns, that call for fast paddling and good steering. So this one might be for the more intermediate to advanced canoe crowd rather than for beginners.

Among the best canoeing with your own boat is on the 182-acre Lake Zumbra in the Carver Park Reserve (access off State Highway 5 on Park Drive). A large waterfowl refuge area is located there, and you will probably spot Canada geese and mallards. Another good lake for paddling and puddling about on a warm summer afternoon is the 162-acre Lake Auburn, also in Carver Park. Small inlets protect you from the wind, and there won't be a fleet of motorboats to chop up your path. Auburn offers great fishing for northern pike. Access is via Carver Park Road off County Highway 11.

The following other natural areas make for some of the best walkabouts in the county.

Baker Park Reserve

Baker Park Reserve has a woodsy public campground with 210 sites, swimming beaches, fishing and boating on three lakes, and executive- and regulation-length golf courses for the duffer set. But the 10 kilometers of hiking/biking paths and 11½ kilometers of cross-country ski trails through the meadows and oak forest make the best reason for visiting Baker Lake. You can walk or jog all day and not have to worry about clutches of roller skaters zooming past or yelling kids playing polo on mountain bikes (as wonderful as both are). The entrance to the campground is near the junction of State Highway 29 (north of U.S. Route 12) and County Highways

19 and 24. Look for Lake Independence on the west side of 19 for a reference, if necessary.

For more information: Call 612-479-2473.

Carver Park Reserve

Carver Park Reserve is a 3,300-acre expanse of wood and prairie, just west of Chanhassen. The Lowry Nature Center on the reserve grounds offers extensive programs, from stargazing in the summer to maple syrup making in the winter. A boardwalk takes visitors through the marsh and tamarack swamp, allowing you to get a good up-close idea about bug, fish, and reptile life. Bike and ski rentals are available or bring your own for use on the 13.7 kilometers of paved biking and hiking trails or the 20½ kilometers of cross-country ski trails. There are an extra 19½ kilometers of turf hiking (no bikes, of course).

For more information: Call the nature center at 612-472-4911 for the latest on programs. The main gate number is 612-446-9474.

Crow-Hassan Park Reserve

Imagine that you are in a covered wagon crossing the Great Plains. That's the impression you get visiting Crow-Hassan Park Reserve, west of Rogers. Just squint your eyes, turn back your mind, and light up your imagination. The 2,600-acre park is a restored prairie, rolling over hills with a carpet of wild grasses and flowers unmatched elsewhere in the metro area. All you need is Ward Bond, of the old *Wagon Train* television show, saying "head 'em up!" Hiking and horseback riding are allowed on 19 kilometers of trails, with skiing on 17.6

kilometers of groomed track. On the weekends in the winter, a warming house at the trailhead offers visitors much-needed concessions.

For more information: Call 612-428-2765.

Elm Creek Park Preserve

The largest of the Hennepin Parks facilities is Elm Creek Park Preserve at 4,900 acres. Entrance to the site is via Territorial Road off County Highway 81 northwest of Osseo. The park is crisscrossed by numerous streams and dotted with ponds and marshes that allow peeks at beavers, wood ducks, herons, and other water critters. Cross-country skiing, biking, and hiking trails are open year-round. The Eastman Nature Center has numerous programs for kids and adults.

For more information: Call 612-424-5511 (park) or 612-420-4300 (nature center).

Fish Lake Regional Park

The 160 acres around Fish Lake Regional Park, just off Bass Lake Road west of I-494, are great for a challenging early-morning or evening hike. Numerous hills make for thigh-strengthening strolls, so be prepared to puff once the steam pressure builds up in your system. The park is well developed, however, with volleyball courts and horseshoe pits, along with public and group picnic areas. Each July an in-line skating festival is held, attracting dozens of skaters. So don't come to Fish Lake expecting to see herds of buffalo. But by arriving early or late, you'll miss most of the crowds. The one-and-one-tenth-mile Glacial Ridge Trail can be accessed from the north or south parking lot. The seven-tenths-of-a-mile

Drumlin Trail skirts a marsh, with access from the south parking lot.

Where: 14512 Bass Lake Road, Maple Grove.
For more information: Call 612-420-3423.

Clifton E. French Regional Park

Canoeing adventures lure outdoors enthusiasts to French Regional Park on Medicine Lake, with its entrance off County Highway 9 about a half mile east of I-494. A self-guided canoe trail through the lake backwaters gets you close to muskrats, egrets, and herons. Toss in a line for panfish and bass. There are more than 11 kilometers of turf hiking trails, plus groomed and lighted cross-country ski trails. A free shuttle tram runs throughout the summer between the visitors-center parking lot and the beach. The Hennepin Parks office is located at French, with a small gift shop there. After a day of play drop by and say hello to the park personnel and thank 'em for a job well done.

For more information: Call 612-559-8891.

Hyland Lake Park Reserve

Hyland Lake Park Reserve is an interesting combination of development (especially the one-acre monster creative play area that even oldsters such as myself love) and naturalness. It epitomizes the 80-20 theory of land use emphasized by Hennepin Parks. The park attracts almost a half million people a year, hardly noticeable on the 1,000 acres because of the spread-out nature of the facility. To find the park office, picnic areas, playgrounds, and paddleboat rentals on Hyland Lake, exit at the park entrance on County Highway 28, about a half mile north of County Highway 1. The Richardson Nature Center is about a mile farther north on 28. It is hard to believe there is such an oasis of quiet surrounded by the Twin Cities suburb of Bloomington. To keep the property pristine, "there is extensive natural resource management here," emphasized park supervisor John Elholm. This includes a 600-acre prairie restoration within the borders of the park and regular plantings of native species flora.

Jane Votca, interpretive naturalist at the Richardson Nature Center, leads numerous programs for school kids throughout the year. "We ask them to sit and listen to the sounds . . . to tell us what they hear. This can be really uncomfortable for a lot of city kids who aren't used to this. Once they leave the parking lot, they think there are bears," she offered. But after a few minutes, Votca can get even a passel of timorous tykes involved in the poetry of the moment, often by simply having pavement-hard youngsters intently touch a leaf. After such a session the children are asked what they have learned about animals' survival needs for food, water, shelter, and space. And the question naturally evolves into what the kids need for themselves on both the physical and emotional levels.

"We often talk about how they can achieve their potential. I hold up a chain and show them how everything in the ecosystem is linked. I say that you may not like something, but you must respect it, because we are all in this world together," said Votca, explaining how she gets the kids to think of broader life issues.

For more information: Call 612-941-7993 to set up a field trip to learn about buzzing bees, incredible insects, animal homes, or what makes a bird a bird. Costs will vary per leader for a naturalist-led program. Call 612-941-4362 to ask about bike and canoe rentals or 612-559-6700 for picnic area or camping reservations and bus information.

Hours: The park office is open from 9:00 A.M. to 9:00 P.M. in the summer months and from 10:00 A.M. to 5:00 P.M. in the winter.

Murphy-Hanrehan Park Reserve

Yeeooooow! The definite adrenaline rush of skiing or mountain biking in the rough terrain of Murphy-Hanrehan Park Reserve is worth every jolt of abject fear shocking your psyche. This 2,400-acre preserve in northwest Scott County (administered by the Scott-Hennepin Park Advisory Board) has three major trail loops that do double duty for intermediate and expert cross-country skiers and mountain bikers. Each loop is a bone cruncher, spine tingler, scalp prickler, and tummy turner. The outer loop, a 10.4-kilometer jog, is the toughest, although the three-kilometer short loop and the six-kilometer interior loop both have enough drop-offs and sharp angles to turn anyone's remaining hair blizzard white— especially when careening down a 70-degree slope on two skinny sticks. As one park worker said, "Next-door Cleary Park is manicured deluxe. Murphy-Hanrehan is just like God made it."

There is no development except for the trails, although a small hut at the trailhead on County Highway 74, which bisects the park, does have a phone. In the winter hot beverages can be purchased there. The hut is open from 3:00 to 5:00 P.M. daily and from 9:00 A.M. to 5:00 P.M. on weekends during ski season.

No park personnel are on duty so skiers and bikers are encouraged not to travel alone in case of accidents. Rangers will come and help, but remember that they aren't simply sitting around next door waiting for your emergency call. You will have to get off the trail, make your way to the trailhead hut, and dial 911. Then wait for rescuers. This is certainly one of the most-challenging tracks within the state, often used for Olympic training. However, be advised that skiing is at the mercy of the weather. In some years there are only four or five days in the entire season that are any good for schussing. The steep slopes and other protected areas sometimes do not receive much snow, and the raw wind whips what is left from the sharp ridgelines. So it is always best to call ahead for trail reports (Cleary Park, call 612-447-2171). But when the winter cooperates, Murphy-Hanrehan cannot be beaten.

Mountain biking is allowed only from August through October, in an effort to limit potential erosion. The bikes have been known to chew up the same tracks used by skiers. Horseback riders have their own 15.6 kilometers of trail opportunities through the hardwood forest.

Don't bypass the park simply because skiing is for the higher level of adventurer, as in the Indiana Jones category. Selfguided wildflower tours are encouraged, which seems like an anomaly when talking about seemingly life-challenging bike rides and skiing in the same breath as the tender spring beauty of a jack-in-the-pulpit. Yet with proper hiking boots, you can have a great time observing the flora. Skip the boutique brands of shoes and get something with high ankle supports and tough soles. Clunky can still be cool, as well as save you from a twisted ankle. Keep an eye open for big-leaf asters and white snakeroot in the autumn, bergamot and Indian pipe in the summer, blood-root and trillium in the spring. I recommend the two-mile-long Wood Duck Trail, accessed from the trailhead park entrance. It offers hilly turf trekking through thick stands of oak. The trail is open year-round (so stay off the nearby mountain bike path).

Where: You can secure a map entitled *Regional Parks* from the Metropolitan Council, Mears Park Centre, 230 East Fifth Street, St. Paul, MN 55101-1626. Call 651-291-6359. The guide covers parks and trails throughout the Twin Cities metro area, including the cities of Bloomington, Minneapolis, and St. Paul, as well as Carver, Dakota, Hennepin, and Washington Counties.

For more information: Hennepin Parks' activities, call 612-559-9000 or use 612-559-6719 for telephone service for the deaf.

Hours: Central office hours are 8:00 A.M. to 4:30 P.M., Monday through Friday. On weekends, park information can be obtained by phoning the individual parks. A free flier listing all the facilities and their contact numbers is available in the information racks in park offices. A trail-information hot line gives a recorded message on trail conditions and trail closings or construction. Call 612-559-6778. Call 612-559-6721 for program information. Website: www.hennepinparks.org.

Pets: Pets are restricted to designated trails and campgrounds. Keep them away from beaches, picnic areas, and paved trails or ski areas. However there are dog exercise and training areas so Fido and Spot can have a free-wheeling romp at Elm Creek Park and Crow-Hassan Park Reserve and Lake Rebecca Regional Park. These are the only places in the system where pets can be free of a leash. You must display a special parking permit to use these sites ($25.00 a year). For more information, call 612-559-6700. For locations of winter pet trails, call 612-559-9000. And don't forget: Clean up after your animals!

Other: There is a daily parking fee of $5.00 to use the Hennepin Parks system. A $25.00 Parks Patron Package includes an annual parking permit valid for 12 months from the date of purchase. Memberships include a quarterly publication. A permit for a second family car is $10.00 if purchased with the first permit or $15.00 if purchased at another time. To encourage everyone to use the parks, residents on economic assistance plans can get help for parking fees through a co-op agreement with Hennepin and Scott Counties. Additional fees are sometimes charged for various programs, so call the park district with any questions. The first Tuesday of every month is a free day when parking fees are waived. For Parks Patron Package information, call 612-559-9000 on weekdays. When a park gate is unattended, use the parking-fee drop box there.

Canoe rentals are available at several of the parks for park-patron rates of $2.00 per half hour (day rate is $20.00). Otherwise rentals are $3.00 per half hour and $25.00 per day. A driver's license or photo identification is required for deposit. Each rental includes paddles and life jackets. Call 612-559-6700 for more information on the Hennepin Parks canoe program and location of rentals.

You may wish to donate to the Forests Forever program within Hennepin Parks. For each $15.00 gift the parks department will plant a 6- to 10-foot-tall native tree in honor of someone you name. For $200 or more a donor can select a more mature tree, help select the planting site, and take part in a planting ceremony. Gifts of $500.00 or more can also be made to the landscape planting fund. In each circumstance donor names are recorded in the Forests Forever permanent log. For details contact the Hennepin Parks Foundation, 12615 County Road 9, Plymouth, MN 55441-1299. Call 612-476-4663.

Ramsey County

Larry Holmberg is a proud guy. He should be, as supervisor of planning and development for the Ramsey County Parks and Recreation Department. He sat in a meeting room at the park offices on North Van Dyke Street in eastern Ramsey County, discussing the challenges and opportunities confronting his unit. He pointed out that there were some 6,000 acres of jewellike parks and recreational areas within the county, which is the smallest in the state and the most heavily populated.

The county sprawls over 103,923 acres (170.2 square miles), with a population of 485,765. Within that area are 82 lakes, helping the state live up to its reputation as a land of 10,000 lakes. Or is it a million? I never could get that right. St. Paul is the largest city, with 272,235 residents. More trivia for the record: The county was founded in 1849 and named after Alexander Ramsey, the first governor of the Minnesota Territory. And some 3,000 volunteers help the county with numerous programs, many of which have to do with environmental and outdoors issues and programs. The county leaves organized sports up to the city recreation department.

Starting work with the parks department in the early 1970s, Holmberg has seen the growth of the system and a need for dealing with the increased demands on the county's greenery. The recreation department, which was started in 1909, began seriously acquiring land in 1914, mainly for building golf courses. By the 1950s, it was purchasing land for swimming beaches, picnicking, and other recreational developments. Afraid that strip malls and tract housing would soon gobble up every available open inch of remaining countryside, the state legislature allowed the county to issue bonds for the acquisition of parklands in 1967. In 1968 the Ramsey County Outdoor Recreation Plan went into effect, recommending environmental corridors and further acquisition. Yet well-meaning proponents of more ice-hockey arenas won out in some circumstances. A legislative battle continued, joined by landowners who wanted free rein to develop property any way they wanted. Arguments flew over disbursement of the few funds available for land purchase. The county was worried that wetlands, steep slope areas, and natural drainage sites would disappear unless steps were taken to save them.

Numerous government agencies banded together to push for a metro acquisition plan, a measure signed into law in 1974, implementing a regional park system. Under the program, greater land management cooperation went into effect for Ramsey, along with its adjacent counties and all their metro governments.

In 1992 Ramsey became the first charter county in the state, which gave it more local control on land use. In 1994 the county board ruled that any disposal of park property has to be replaced with land comparable in size and quality. Eighty-five percent of the county residents voiced their support for such a plan, Holmberg said.

"A lot of residents like that natural area around their homes," he offered. However the shrinking of available open space continues to bring the community into fierce confrontation with developers and builders. In the mid-1990s such a problem developed over six acres of Arden Hills adjacent to a park in the northwestern part of the county. The privately owned land eventually was sold for a housing tract over loud neighborhood protests.

A battle over use of the abandoned 2,500-acre Twin Cities Army Ammunition Plant was raging at the time of this writing, with development plans thicker than fleas on road kill. Included in the area is a 1,000-acre wetland that is appreciated by travel-weary, migrating waterfowl. The four square miles of hills, prairies, and empty parking lots had been an ammo manufacturing plant during World War II and now sits mostly vacant.

"We also have concerns over wildlife, especially with an abundance of deer," Holmberg said ruefully, citing the problem that comes with one wild creature readily adapting to urbanization. "Having them hit by cars is not a good way to control the population."

Strolling along the edges of the county's lakes, pausing amid the pine groves, or watching a Canada goose fly by makes all these problems drift away on the poetry of the day. Amid the city clamor, there are nature's getaways. They make the preservation fight all the more worthwhile.

Lake Vadnais

Take the unnamed road between the east and west sections of 1,200-acre Lake Vadnais, between County Road F and Vadnais Boulevard, and observe the 50-foot-high red pines that

A Common Loon

rim the shoreline. The trees were planted in the 1940s around Vadnais, a natural reservoir for the county's water supply. Gilfillan Park, a quiet, small picnic area at Sucker Lake just north of Vadnais, is a place where kids can watch the ducks or do some shore fishing. The 30-acre park is one-quarter mile east of Rice Street, south of State Highway 96. There are more natural areas available for hiking and wildlife study on the north side of Lake Vadnais by taking County Road F east of Rice Street or to Vadnais Lake South via Vadnais Boulevard east of Rice Street.

Battle Creek Regional Park

Battle Creek Regional Park (with parking for 270 cars) is in southern Maplewood east of McKnight Road, between I-94 and Upper Afton Road. The 1,840-acre park is a welcome respite amid the sprawl. The woods, grassland, and marsh areas are home to many varieties of wildlife, including egrets, deer, and foxes. Some of the more developed areas include a 500-person group picnic pavilion with kitchens, an area for weekly summer concerts, and walking trails to get away from that mob.

For more information: Call 651-748-2500 for information.

Bald Eagle Park and Otter Lake Regional Park

Bald Eagle Park and Otter Lake Regional Park consist of 884 acres in White Bear Township in the far northeast corner of the county. Surrounded by suburban clusters, the parks are some of the last remaining large natural areas west of U.S. Route 61 in the metro area. Exit the highway at Buffalo Street, turn west and pick up Bald Eagle Boulevard which rims the south and west sides of Bald Eagle Lake. Deer, foxes, owls, bluebirds, otters—you name it, and Bald Eagle has it. Even osprey have been seen hunkering into the reedy areas of Bald Eagle Lake and nearby Otter Lake on the west side of the park property. You can get to the Otter Lake unit by taking Otter Lake Road north from State Highway 96. On the way you will pass Birch Lake and the Tamarack Lake Nature Preserve.

For more information: Call 651-748-2500.

Tamarack Nature Center

Speaking of the Tamarack Nature Center, this is a must stop on any tour of the county's parklands. The center is a 320-acre preserve located within the Bald Eagle-Otter Lakes Regional Park. Meandering wood-chip trails and boardwalks make for easy hiking and are readily accessible for the physically challenged.

There is a half-mile bituminous-path loop specifically designed for wheelchair access. A dock extends out onto Tamarack Lake so youngsters can get a great view of water life. It's also a good place from which to watch herons and other waterbirds doing their dipping-and-diving dances. In the winter there is a groomed four-and-a-half-mile cross-country ski trail, with rentals and lessons available. The nature center offers puppet shows, pond studying, maple syrup manufacturing, and other kid-neat activities in its urban surroundings.

Many schools and community groups use the preserve for nature studies. Along with birthday parties, summer day camps, and evening and weekend programs, the place is hoppier than a rabbit on a hot grate.

Where: The center is bounded by Otter Lake Road (east), County Road H-2 (north), I-35E (west), and Hammond Road (south) at 5287 Otter Lake Road in White Bear Lake. Parking is off Otter Lake Road.

For more information: Call 651-470-5350. Trail hours are daily from a half hour before sunrise to a half hour after sunset.

Hours: Tamarack is open from 8:30 A.M. to 5:00 P.M., Monday through Saturday and from noon to 5:00 P.M., Sunday.

State Capitol Mall

State Capitol Mall is aptly named Minnesota's front yard. Okay so it isn't located in the woods, but the grassy expanse provides a comforting spot for bare feet in the summer. It offers a peek at spring flowers, a chance to ogle autumn colors, and the opportunity to escape a confining office and enjoy wintertime fresh air. The 36-acre green space links the capitol building with the state office building, the judicial building, and the Minnesota History Center (on John Ireland Boulevard). The site is dotted with memorials, including those honoring Minnesota's Vietnam vets and Minnesota's own Lone Eagle, trans-Atlantic flier Charles A. Lindbergh. The area is host to the Taste of Minnesota food festival and Winter Carnival activities, as well as being the finish line for the Twin Cities Marathon. Even with all these hyperactive doin's, I suggest you halt for a minute and smell the roses (in the little garden on the south end of the mall near the Court of Honor plaza).

Harriet Island/Lilydale Regional Park

Harriet Island/Lilydale Regional Park is on the Mississippi River across from downtown St. Paul. Until 1950 this was a true island but the 200-foot-wide channel was filled in then to link the dot of ground to the mainland. While most of the "island" is now home to developed recreation areas (ball fields, playgrounds, and picnic sites), there is a two-and-a-half-mile-long and half-mile-wide preserve with 100 acres of marsh and woods. Lilydale, which once housed an often river-socked cluster of homes, is now a cleared flood plain. It was also the site of the Twin City Brick Co., which dug out clay along the river banks for almost 100 years before closing. The gouging exposed fossil beds, making it still a favorite among pro and amateur paleontologists.

Long Lake Regional Park

Long Lake, made up of 217 acres, is located in New Brighton on the county's northwestern side. The surrounding park includes one and a half miles of shoreline around the lake and a natural preserve along Rush Lake which includes a cattail marsh, oak woods, and nine acres of restored prairie. Three miles of hiking and biking trails make their way around the lakes. Be aware, however, that the beach is open for swimming from Memorial Day through Labor Day, and the concession stands can be jammed. There are also picnic areas with volleyball courts, playing fields, and a handicapped-accessible play area.

Hidden Falls/Crosby Regional Park

Crosby Farm is named after an English immigrant in the 1850s who staked out a land claim in the river valley southwest of what is today's junction of Shepard Road and I-35E. Great pan fishing can be had in Upper and Lower Crosby Lakes. A nature center is on the grounds, as well as six and seven-tenths miles of trails running along the heavily wooded river bottoms. Sailboats and motorboats bob at anchor in Watergate

Marina, located between Crosby Farm and the Hidden Falls section of the park. Many schools use the parkland for handy-to-reach outdoor classrooms for nature studies. Cross-country skiers love the 13.9 kilometers of ground trails whenever the season turns its thoughts to polar bears.

For more information: Call the nature center at 612-929-6548 (phone and fax).

Keller-Phalen and Como Regional Parks

Other parks, such as Keller-Phalen and Como, are more geared to recreational opportunities than emphasizing a more nature-oriented getaway. But don't pass them up because of this. The Keller unit of Keller-Phalen has picnic sites and boat launches at Kohlman, Gervais, Spoon, Keller, and Round Lakes. A mile of paved walking paths connects the various segments of the park and connects with the 18-mile-long Willard Munger State Trail.

The latter runs from St. Paul to Pine Point Park, four miles north of Stillwater. The Phalen unit contains St. Paul's only swimming lake, but don't get nibbled by the walleye and northern pike that also call the place their home. There are extensive hiking and biking trails through the groomed setting, in addition to great golfing. Como Regional Park offers an 18-hole golf course, a zoo, a conservatory, and a lake for paddleboating.

For more information: Ramsey County Parks and Recreation Department, 2015 North Van Dyke Street, Maplewood, MN 55109-3796. Call 651-748-2500.

Other: Paved hiking and biking trails are located in Battle Creek, Keller, Long Lake, and Snail Lake Regional Parks, and at Island Lake County Park. Four trails connect with other regional parks: Rice Creek West, Rice Creek North, Birch Lake, and Burlington-Northern. The county offers 22 miles of groomed ski trails in the winter, located in the five regional parks and at Manitou Ridge Golf Course. Remember that a Minnesota cross-country ski license is required and may be purchased at Tamarack Nature Center or park offices.

Minnesota Valley
National Wildlife Refuge

It is hard to believe the Mall of America is within a few blocks of stepping through the door of one of the best natural hideaways in the Twin Cities area. The massive shopping mall with its sprawling concrete and neon rears its contemporary urban head along Killibrew Drive, south of I-494 between Cedar Avenue and 24th Avenue. With me on a visit to the refuge was 14-year-old nephew Joe, who in his decade and a half of life has seen almost all the green space of his Bloomington hometown disappear under pavement. So he was definitely impressed that bald eagles and osprey could live that close to a monolith, one complete with an indoor Ferris wheel and enough shoe stores to outfit more than a dozen dictators' wives.

Bypassing the glitzy retailing temple, we visited the Minnesota Valley National Wildlife Refuge one windy rain-swept Sunday morning in early May. Crowds were starting to pile up at the entrance ramps to the mall's formidable multi-tier parking structure as we turned off Old Shakopee Road and drove past a flock of sheep (really!) grazing at Spruce Shadows Farm. Turning right on East 80th Street, we wound our way around the rear of the Airport Hilton Hotel. The visitors center is tucked behind a grove of trees and prairie-grass plantings. The sheep would have loved the quiet and the tall grass. Most of the mall-ites never knew the refuge was there.

The visitors center and main office of the refuge, administered by the U.S. Fish and Wildlife Service, have a modernistic feel. But history inspired the design, using local kasota stone, cedar shakes, metal, and concrete. The architectural concept was to offer a transition from the surrounding urban environment to a natural landscape. The refuge was established in 1976, proving that wildlife and urban areas can coexist if each does its job properly. The mission of the refuge is to protect and maintain the resources there. It is also there to ensure the diversity of the valley's habitat in eight management units, four of which have interpretive trails and signs. More than 340 species of mammals, reptiles, birds, and amphibians call the valley home, as well as dozens of plant varieties.

One of only four urban wildlife refuges in the country, the 34-mile, 9,500-acre corridor stretches from Bloomington to Jordan along the Minnesota River bottomlands. The other urban refuges are Bayou Savage near New Orleans, John Neinz Natural Wildlife Refuge at Tinicun Marsh near Philadelphia, and the San Francisco Bay National Wildlife Refuge.

The rock outcroppings comprising the Minnesota River's valley walls were formed a billion years ago as part of what geologists call the Canadian Shield. The formation extends from northern and eastern Canada to the far prairies of southwestern Minnesota. The bedrock is generally hidden under a rich, thick layer of glacial deposits. However in the upper Minnesota River valley, this covering was stripped away by the rushing waters of melting glaciers around 9000 B.C. The water formed an inland sea larger than all the Great Lakes combined. After a thousand years the waters of a dam made of glacial rubble broke and created a mighty river, which carved out a plain one to four miles in width and more than 300 feet deep. The Minnesota River valley is the legacy of that mighty flood.

Displays within the center attracted Joe's attention, tracing the role that men and women played in changing that eons-old landscape to their needs. The center is the best place to start any visit to the valley. Above each lighted exhibit, sound effects create a realistic backdrop. The soft sighing of wind and bird calls from the early days melts into the harsh sound of axes and the cry of roosters and chickens to denote settlement. According to the refuge staff, almost three million people live within an hour's drive of the valley today. The influx means that there remains only 20 percent of the wetlands of Carver, Dakota, Hennepin, and Scott Counties. Highways, airports, parking lots, malls, and housing have gobbled the rest. More than half of the original 215 million acres of wetlands have been drained and filled. There are 56 storm sewers carrying water directly into the refuge. The Minnesota River valley watershed is also affected by more than 40,000 individual landowners who contribute to a runoff of silt, agricultural pollutants, and assorted other waste.

Panels trace the demise of the woodlands, showing how the refuge lies in a transition zone between prairie and forest. Another great display is a magnifying glass suspended by a string in front of a towering aquarium. By using the glass guests can see up close the plant life and fish in the tank. An extensive book shop in the center is valuable for stocking up on the state's outdoors scene, with hints on canoeing, biking, and camping. Be sure to take in the 12-minute audiovisual show that can be viewed from the comfort of an auditorium. It was a perfect place to hole up until the drizzle halted outside. A fieldstone hearth, ringed by cushioned stone benches near the building entrance, is fired up in the winter. This creates a marvelous winter nook for cozy storytelling.

Joe and I then explored the half-mile-long Hillside Trail near the building, as the wind rustled through the waist-high bluestem prairie grass. A rooster pheasant cawed in the distance, while several robins offered observations on the day from their perch in a nearby maple. The trail offers a strenuous climb from the bluff down to the observation point near Petterson Pond on the valley floor. The hike is not recommended for individuals with heart problems—the reason is easy to see. The return trek is equivalent to walking up the stairs in a 12-story building. Around the visitors center is the Bluff Prairie restoration, once an old lawn, now restored to native grasses and wildflowers. A free 40-minute tape, along with tape recorder, can be checked out in the office for a quick self-guided bird-watching tour on the Hillside Trail and the Bluff Prairie.

Quick trips to the refuge can satisfy the need for green space. A solid hour in the visitors center provides plenty of background on the first visit. A two-hour block gets visitors back and forth to the Bass Ponds Environmental Area, and a half-day excursion is good for the pristine prairie at the Black Dog Preserve in Burnsville. Black Dog was a Sioux leader in the 1850s whose summer camp was on the northeastern shore of Black Dog Lake.

We found other highlights within the refuge. Long Meadow Lake, with its 2,200 acres of bluff, hardwood forests, and fields, is accessible via five miles of hiking and cross-country ski trails (not maintained, however).

Louisville Swamp consists of 2,400 acres of marsh and bottomlands packed with birds, frogs, and fish. Thirteen miles of trails accommodate hikers, bikers, horseback riders, and skiers. The 4½-mile Mazomani Trail (named for another early

Native American leader) is one of the best in the refuge. The trail angles southwest for about a quarter mile along the edge of a prairie before ascending to a bluff. You can then walk along the ridge, descend again to the bottomland forest, and cross a bridge over Sand Creek. Look for the erratic, large, glacial boulder dumped there eons ago. On the walk there are plenty of opportunities to spot toads, wood frogs, red foxes, muskrats, and skunks. The Wilke section of the reserve is home to a great blue heron rookery, which means that the area's hiking trails are closed during the spring baby-raising season. Look for signage.

The 380-acre Bloomington Ferry river crossing, Upgrala's 2,400 acres of forested riverbanks below Eden Prairie, and Chaska Lake's flood plain have no public access, although they are part of the refuge.

Ed Moyer, a refuge interpreter, shook his head when explaining the ever-changing nearby landscape. "No one ever envisioned a mega-mall here that attracts 38 to 40 million people a year. But I guess shopping is the world's largest recreational activity." Occasionally the center has exhibits at the mall in an effort to show the resources next door to the concrete. Almost 40,000 visitors come to the center every year, while an estimated 173,000 use the corridor. "That's hard to measure," Moyer explained, "due to so many entry points."

"We are trying to preserve a bit of the real world. We are really pro-life out here," Moyer indicated, describing the refuge's efforts in land management and wildlife protection. He said that the refuge works with area schools and teachers in an outreach program. "Teachers are then really prepared to reach out to the youngsters."

The refuge is undergoing welcome additions. In early 1995, the U.S. Fish and Wildlife Service secured the Mud Lake Waterfowl Production Area, a 298-acre tract south of Green Isle, which was purchased from the proceeds of the sale of federal duck stamps. The wetlands around that lake drain into the Minnesota River. Another acquisition added 1,500 acres in Carver County, across the river from the Louisville Swamp unit and the Carver Rapids unit of the Minnesota Valley State Park. The addition contains a 200-acre lake and a native prairie and oak savanna never touched by farmers' plows. This unit opened to the public in 1997, following restoration of some abandoned farm fields to prairie status.

Where: To get to the Minnesota Valley National Wildlife Refuge visitors center from I-494, exit at 34th Avenue South. Turn left at the Holiday Inn and go about one-quarter mile to 3815 East 80th Street. To get to Bass Ponds from Cedar Avenue/State Highway 77, exit on Old Shakopee Road. Go east to 86th Street and turn right. From the visitors center turn left at the gate and left again at the next three traffic lights.

There are three trailheads at the Black Dog Preserve. From I-35W exit on Cliff Road, go east for a half mile to the Metro Transit park-and-ride lot. You can park near the soccer fields there and walk around the pitch to an information kiosk just to the north. The second trailhead is reached from State Highway 13 in Burnsville. Drive north and west on River Hills Drive to Radisson Drive. Turn right on Radisson, and follow it down the hill to the park sign. Near the kiosk there is a path that leads over a pedestrian bridge above the railroad tracks. From there enter the preserve. The last trailhead is reached via I-35W on the Black Dog Road exit. Drive east about two miles to the parking lot, which is west of the Northern States Power Company plant.

To reach Louisville Swamp from Shakopee, go south on U.S. Route 169 about 4½ miles. Turn right onto 145th Street, follow the road past the main entrance to the Renaissance

Festival (watch out for knight and minstrel crossings), and proceed over the railroad tracks. A parking lot is on the left. The Wilke unit of the refuge is reached from I-35W on the State Highway 13 South exit (as you aim toward Shakopee). Drive straight ahead on State Highway 13 until it becomes State Highway 101. Go a half mile west of the County Highway 18/State Highway 101 intersection, and look for a sign depicting a wood duck.

For more information: Minnesota Valley National Wildlife Refuge, 3815 East 80th Street, Bloomington, MN 55425-1600. Call 612-335-2323 (visitors center); Friends of the Minnesota Valley, Box 20244, Bloomington, MN 55420 (information about volunteer efforts in the valley).

Pets: Not recommended and should definitely be leashed.

Other: The Minnesota Nature Photography Club meets at the refuge offices. The group is affiliated with the Photographic Society of America and the Twin Cities Area Council of Camera Clubs. Field trips, workshops, photo competitions, and other activities are held regularly, with meetings on the third Wednesday of the month from September through May. For more information, call Ron Cleveland at 612-425-6009. Area camera clubs also have a Web page that links with each organization: www.cameracouncil.org.

Fort Snelling State Park

Glacial deposits and meltwater erosion were the two major factors that fashioned the landscape of Fort Snelling State Park. Moraines, ridges of rubble left along the rim of departing glaciers, gave a ripple effect to ground atop the bedrock throughout the area. Then the runoff from the melting ice dug deeply into the sediment to create cliffs hundreds of feet high, scouring out the beds of the Mississippi, the Minnesota, and the St. Croix Rivers.

Heavily forested, the region was rich in game. The rivers were thick with fish. Numerous Native American nations came and went, their passage not even disturbing the aspen and willow that clustered along the river bottoms. Among the Native tribes were the Chippewa, or Ojibway, eventually to be edged out by the Dakotas, or *Nadoussioux*, which means "enemy" in Ojibway language. The Dakotas, commonly known as Sioux, were the prime fighting force in the vicinity. Medicine Bottle camped at Pine Bend along the Mississippi River; Black Dog's village lay at a bend of the Minnesota River where today's Burnsville is located; and a camp called Kaposia occupied land where contemporary South St. Paul sprawls.

French traders came and went among the villages but never lingered long. It wasn't until the early 1800s that significant populations of whites were in evidence.

Along came army explorer Zebulon Pike, whose mission was to establish a fort to protect the growing number of Yankees. Putting up his travel-stained canvas tents on Pike Island, he met with the Dakotas and negotiated a land transfer to allow use of land for his encampment. In the early 1800s two sites were developed. Cantonment New Hope, now Picnic Island, and Camp Coldwater were swampy and disease ridden. As a result the new Fort St. Anthony was constructed on the bluffs overlooking the Mississippi River by engineer Josiah Snelling (in whose honor the fort was eventually named). I've always wondered why the original fortifications weren't built on the higher, drier site in the first place. It seems to me that it would have saved the lives of many unfortunate fever victims who had to endure damp sleeping bags and attacks by nasty mosquitoes.

But as they say, history rolls on. The fort grew in importance and became the trading and cultural center of the Minnesota territory, as well as its military base. The first school in the state was opened there in 1823, as well as the first library and the first hospital. The first Protestant church in Minnesota held services within the walls.

Yet perhaps more importantly for outdoors enthusiasts, one of the early post commanders directed the first natural resource management project in the region. He built Minnesota's first sawmill and gristmill, using the raging power of St. Anthony's Falls.

Today the mills are long gone, disappearing under the weight of contemporary times. The Twin Cities grew and grew, like the proverbial Topsy. However, the river bottomlands and the islands remained as refuges for Twin Citians seeking a respite from the rush of modern living. On the hilltop overlooking the Mississippi and Minnesota Rivers, are polo grounds and a golf course. The fort still stands as formidable as ever there. The site is now managed by the Minnesota Historical Society as a living-history museum. Men and women interpreters are garbed in military and civilian clothing of the early 1800s, adapting their speech and presentation to that era. It is easy to turn the mental clock back six generations to those days just by walking in the front gate. One rainy autumn Sunday, when it was too sloshy to roam the bottomlands, I had several hours of delightful conversation with characters from another era. They stayed true to their researched roles throughout my entire stay.

Yet it is down in the valley where that getaway feeling is even more obvious. Silver maple, green ash, elm, and cottonwoods line the riverbanks in a lush spread of greenery, which in autumn is a rainbow blast of shimmering crimson and gold. Cautious white-tailed deer scoot in and out of the brush for dawn and evening feedings, but they can be spotted if you sit quietly. Skunks, badgers, and other animals also call the area their home, with the grass and marsh plants around Gun Club Lake the best from which to observe them. Turtles of all types (snappers, soft-shellers, and woodies) hang out on semi-submerged logs or sun themselves, doing their lazy *Testudinidae* thing.

A year-round naturalist leads interpretive programs regularly from the visitors center, with hikes and programs throughout the park. The trails connect on the north to Minnehaha Park upriver along the Mississippi. You may even want to try one of the guided wintertime snowshoe treks through the park grounds.

The 18 miles of scenic hiking trails do double duty for cross-country skiing when Minnesota's frosty January breath whips up knee-deep drifts of North Country snow. On more balmy days you can launch your canoe on the south end of Snelling Lake and from behind the park office onto the Minnesota River.

Back in the days when I was hitchhiking home to Iowa from my days at the then College (now University) of St. Thomas in St. Paul, I would often stand at the end of the Mendota Bridge while waiting for rides. The structure spanned the deep river valley where the park is located, and I always wondered what was down there. Years later I knew enough to go down and find out. At first while down in the valley, it seems odd to have a bridge overhead, you soon lose the sense that the roadway is there. It just doesn't matter amid the rushes and reeds that traffic is racing past high above you.

Where: Act like an explorer from the good old *voyageur* era. Simply follow the signs. Fort Snelling State Park is in the heart of the Twin Cities metroplex with the park entrance off State Highway 5 at Post Road near the Minneapolis–St. Paul International Airport.

For more information: Fort Snelling State Park Manager, Highway 5 and Post Road, St. Paul, MN 55111. Call 612-726-2389; Department of Natural Resources, Division of Parks and

Recreation Information Center, 500 Lafayette Road, St. Paul, MN 55155-4040. Call 651-296-6157 or 800-646-6367 and ask for the DNR.

Hours: Park gates are open from 8:00 A.M. to 10:00 P.M. Historic Fort Snelling is open Monday through Saturday from 9:30 A.M. to 5:00 P.M. and Sunday from 11:30 A.M. to 5:00 P.M., May through October. The interpretive center is open year-round. Call 612-725-2413 for recorded information. Museum hours are 10:00 A.M. to 5:00 P.M. and Sunday from noon to 5:00 P.M. Gift shop hours are 9:30 A.M. to 5:30 P.M. and Sunday from 11:30 A.M. to 5:00 P.M.

Admission: $5.00, adults 16 to 61; $4.00, seniors; $3.00, children 6 to 15; and free for youngsters 5 and under and members of the Minnesota Historical Society. Call 612-726-1171 Tuesday through Friday between 8:30 A.M. and 4:30 P.M. for group rates. Daily or annual permits are required for all vehicles entering the state park, even for hiking in the valley below. Permits are not required at the historical site.

Amenities: The state park has more than 100 picnic sites with two enclosed shelters. There is also a swimming beach, flush toilets, drive-in water access on Picnic Island and at Cedar Avenue. A state park visitors center is located just below the historic site. Call 612-725-2724.

Pets: Must be restrained on a leash.

Best time to visit: Year-round.

Activities: Hiking, biking, skiing, golfing, interpretive center programs, polo, living-history museum, canoeing.

Other: There are special events throughout the season, such as Civil War Weekend, Children's Days, Fur Trade Rendezvous, Music on the U.S. Frontier and other programs.

5

Southwest

For canoeing the far southwest anchor corner of Minnesota is excellent. All access points are easily reached via highway and interstate, with plenty of publicly owned sites for input and egress. There are also numerous opportunities to get onto the best waterways via private lands as well. Respect any posting notices, don't disturb the cows, watch out for barbed-wire fences, and leave the area as undisturbed as you found it. You can also put in near bridges across county roads. But be aware that the steep banks and lack of nearby parking can be a problem.

You won't go wrong with the Minnesota River, a gentle, family-oriented waterway. The flowage offers a delightful panache of scenery, most of it along farmland but with plenty of rock outcroppings for variety from Granite Falls to North Redwood. Most of the river is of the Class I category, meaning there are only easy rapids, minimal wave action, and hardly any obstructions. As such it is a perfect beginners' route or one on which you can take small kids with little worry (remember the life jackets, however).

Yet, even more advanced canoers will have a pleasant experience. There is a brief stretch of white water called Patterson's Rapids near Renville County Park 2, where sparkling water tumbles around some boulders. But apart from that adrenalin rush, the Minnesota River passage is relatively easy to navigate. The park, near the intersection of County Highways 6 and 15, has a campsite and canoe-launch site.

Geologists say that the granite, forming the banks of the river depression, is at least three billion years old. The broad valley was once the bed of the glacial River Warren, named after an army engineer who first officially described the landscape in his reports. The ancient river flowed south out of glacial Lake Agassiz between 9,000 and 12,000 years ago, because all the northern ends were blocked by ice. In today's "new-speak" language, the current Minnesota is called an "underfit" flowage, because it seems to be a mere stream meandering through the broad old valley. In some places the valley is five miles wide, with banks up to 250 feet high. Icy ol' Warren must have been quite a river.

Today the Minnesota is fed by hundreds of smaller rivers and streams, many of them navigable by canoe: Birch Coulee, the Redwood and Yellow Medicine Rivers, and creeks such as Hawk, Crow, Boiling Spring, and Wabasha.

There are only two portages in this stretch of the Minnesota. The first is a distance of about 250 yards around the dam in Granite Falls. You can avoid that if canoeing south by putting in at War Memorial Park on the south side of the city. The next portage is also about 200 yards, circumventing another dam just below the park. Skip both by launching at the junction of County Highways 40 and 52, where there is a campsite.

The forests in the vicinity are comprised of stately elm and maple and fluffy cottonwood. Graceful willows tickle the water surface with the sweeping majesty of their long green fingers. Inland you'll find oak and cedar stands.

The stretch between Granite Falls on the north and Fort Ridgely State Park on State Highway 4 to the south (on the border between Renville and Nicollet Counties) is historically rich but often troubled. Steamboats plied the waterway as early as the 1850s. But the Dakota uprising raged through this part of Minnesota in 1862, putting a halt to river traffic. Despite pleas from their leaders, the government had failed to provide food and supplies to the Native Americans, thus triggering the upheaval.

One trader, Andrew Myrick at the Lower Sioux Agency, said, "If they are hungry, let 'em eat grass." Frustrated, starving, and desperate, the Dakota attacked all those they felt had done them wrong. Myrick was one of the first to be revenged. His body was found later, mouth stuffed with grass. When the violence was over, almost 1,000 whites and unknown numbers of Native Americans were dead. Even when the rebellion was eventually crushed, it was years before the Minnesota River valley was really settled.

You can see remains of trading posts, homesteads, and military encampments along the river, a grim reminder of those tragic early years. Markers at many spots elaborate on the grim details.

The Minnesota River north of Granite Falls to Ortonville provides a different experience for paddlers. Peaceful. Calm. Quiet. Marshy lowlands are at the foot of the granite bluffs, with opportunities for bird-watching. You may even spot some prickly-pear cactus (cactus in Minnesota?) growing in the vicinity, one of nature's many quirks. Watch out for snags, old bridge pilings, and other obstacles along this area. However it is still a Class I flowage.

Big Stone Lake (near the Big Stone National Wildlife Refuge), the Minnesota River Reservoir, Marsh Lake. and Lac qui Parle lake have been formed by dams on the river.

There are access sites at each. Be aware that part of the Lac qui Parle Wildlife Management Area, including Lac qui Parle from the State Highway 40 bridge to the dam, is closed to the public from September 20 to December 1. Wildlife officials do not want the migrating birds to be disturbed during that time. You can make up for that temporary seasonal closure by paddling around the southeast end of Lac qui Parle. The state park there has numerous back channels with a plentiful supply of birds, muskrats, deer, and beavers to observe.

The Des Moines River, which flows from the Gopher State into southern neighbor Iowa, has more rapids than its sister, the Minnesota. But neither is really difficult to traverse. Watch out for dams, logjams, and downed trees. Heavy rains in spring often cause flooding, so avoid the high water whenever possible.

The river corkscrews through the flat plateau, called the *Coteau des Prairies* by early French adventurers. Contemporary travelers will see the same lowlands, now mostly corn and wheat fields and pastures. Few trees break up the broad expanse. From the town of Windom to Kilen Woods State Park, rolling hills undulate off to the horizon. Green ash, elm, and willow break up the sight lines. As you paddle closer to the park, 200-foot-high bluffs rear from the river. Oak and basswood crown the crests, like a full head of green hair. As you move from Kilen Woods south to Jackson, taller hills hide the farms from sight.

Everywhere are hawks, bank swallows, and other birds swooping over the tall grasses. Be sure to bring a fishing pole. Channel catfish, pike, bullheads, and yellow perch are abundant, just waiting to leap into your frying pan—well, almost. You do have to have patience and know when to pull up on the line. Camouflaged turtles loll away their summer afternoons on the logs and mud banks, splashing into the water if startled.

Blue Mounds State Park

A buffalo bull is big—reeeeeeaaaally big. Smelly—reeeeaaally smelly. Moves where it wants to move. Has horns. Doesn't like to be bothered by details. Like humans.

There he was. Eyeball to eyeball with me as the wind rustled through the bluestem prairie grasses. He raised his black, wet nose. Sniffing, the dripping nostrils widened, mucus glistening. Round, brown bovine eyes glinted through a Rastafarian hairdo. The bull looked. Blinked. Lowered his massive head. Resumed brunch. I was inconsequential.

Not that there would have been any real trouble. After all he and his lady friends were inside a bison-proof fence at Blue

Buffalo at Blue Mounds State Park

Mounds State Park. And I was outside the multi-acre enclosure. But being that close to 30-plus animals, who used to call this entire range their home, was certainly exciting.

For the record, the official name of the buffalo is American bison. Each year usually in October, the state's Material Management Division of the Department of Administration auctions off excess animals from the Blue Mounds herd. If you are interested in buying a buffalo/bison and being the envy of your neighbors, call the park offices at 507-283-4892 for the sale details. You won't be taking home a sick animal. They have all been tested for brucellosis, tuberculosis, and anaplasmosis. Health certificates are available upon request. That's often better than what you can get at the local animal shelter with a new puppy. Think of it, no more lawn mowing with one of these critters tethered in front of the house.

The park is a remnant of what once was endless miles of prairie. While homesteaders made short shrift of much of the surrounding landscape, rock outcrops and shallow soil saved most of the earth within what is today's park. Subsequently, it is one of the best places in Minnesota to see what an original prairie—complete with buffalo—would have been generations ago. However, the ground needed restoration, because heavy grazing by domestic animals over the years diminished the native plants. Exotic species then had a chance to spring up and crowd out some of the remaining originals. The state has subsequently needed to transplant and seed areas within the park, to return it to its natural beauty. Controlled fires are often used in this prairie management scheme, stimulating native plant growth and getting rid of species that do not belong. Today a hiker can see dozens of flower and grass species that have "returned home." Spring is the best time for viewing the riot of color, as new buds open. By the end of the growing season, some of the plants, such as the big bluestem, can reach up to seven feet tall.

Sitting atop a quartzite ridge near piles of glacially deposited boulders, a careful observer can see patches of prickly-pear cacti. Blue Mounds State Park is one of the few places in Minnesota where such plants have found a foothold. Be on hand in June and July when the cacti blossom, sprinkling the park's crown with yellow freckles.

This ridge, known as The Mound, has always shimmered on the horizon during the summer's heat. Ox-drawn wagon trains of sod-busting settlers used the easily identifiable landmark while lumbering their way westward. The Mound's hazy blue appearance, rising from its flatiron surroundings, was the perfect directional.

The quartzite eventually became prized as a construction component for buildings in the area. Quarries dating back to the last century can still be viewed on the way to the visitors center. The neighboring town of Luverne seems to have sprung from the living rock, since many of its homes and businesses were built from that massive material. At least the town will never blow away.

In 1937 Mound Creek was dammed to form the lakes that now make up the heart of the park. Originally known as the Mound Springs Recreation Area, the park earned its current name in 1961. In that year the first buffalo were reintroduced, moved there from the Fort Niobrara Wildlife Refuge near Valentine, Nebraska. Several observation platforms overlook the buffalo grazing area, and, while hiking on the ridges, the animals can also be observed. The latter vantage point is the best, because you can get the feel of what was once the immense prairie. Deer, not native to the region, have also found the park's wooded areas to be comfortable hiding places. On otherwise still nights, the cries of coyotes echo over the sleeping land.

The rock formations found in the park are at least 1½ billion years old, starting as the bottom of an ancient sea.

Sandstone, under pressure and chemical reactions, eventually turned into the hard quartzite. Iron oxide causes the purple-blue coloring. While geologists have all that figured out, there is at least one mystery in the park that needs solving. A 1,250-foot-long rock wall, aligned on an east-to-west direction, can be found at the southern end of the park along the Burr Oak Trail. No one knows how that line of stones came to be there. On the first day of spring and fall, however, it is obvious that the sunrise and sunset are perfectly lined up along the rock formation. According to historians and archaeologists, it is neither of Native American nor settler origin. Could it be a roadside marker for space aliens?

That may be the case but noted Minnesota author Frederick Manfred never worried much about a visitor from hyperspace knocking on his door, although the mysterious wall is only several hundred feet from what was his home. Manfred's house, which he used from 1960 to 1975, now doubles as the park's visitors and interpretive center. The author's exciting tales of Native Americans, such as *Wanderlust* and the *Scarlet Plume* collection, line the bookshelves in a circular upper room that serves as an observation deck. Look out over the rolling hills from Manfred's upper room, which he called his "tipi," and soak in the essence of the land that contributed to his creativity.

Where: The 1,500-acre Blue Mounds State Park is located in Rock County six miles north of I-90 and Luverne and 16 miles south of Pipestone in Rock County. The park entrance is off U.S. Route 75.

For more information: Blue Mounds State Park Manager, Rural Route 1, Luverne, MN 56156. Call 507-283-1307.

Amenities: The park has 73 semimodern campsites and 40 with electrical hookups. A trailer dump station is also available. There is a primitive group camp and picnic grounds with a shelter. The swimming beach is along Lower Mound Lake. There are 13 miles of foot trails and seven miles available for snowmobiling.

Pets: Leashed.

Best time to visit: Spring and summer.

Activities: Hiking, swimming, camping, buffalo-watching, fishing, and canoeing.

Other: The rangers, and plenty of signage, warn visitors not to touch or tease the buffalo. Do not enter the grazing area. That bull will not ignore you.

Camden State Park

For the creative mind coming into Camden State Park is like descending into a secret glen inhabited by hobbits, elves, and cousin fairy creatures. The dim, cool valley is an Elsinore, a Brigadoon, a Tir Na nOg where anything delightful can happen amid the maple and basswood groves. Early pioneers thought the same, as they trundled in off the vast prairie. Sunburned, dusty, and tired, the arrivals appreciated the oasis with its fresh spring water, wild game, and protection from what seemed to be the constant wind. Today's state park straddles the summit of the *Couteau des Prairies*, the prairie highlands that separate the Minnesota and Missouri Rivers.

More than a million years ago Pleistocene Age glaciers pancaked the land, with the so-called Des Moines lobe littering the area with voluminous amounts of glacial drift, all that throwaway stuff that had been scraped up on the journey southward. Raging water, caused when the glaciers melted, carved out the valley. The luscious, sweet springs prized by Native Americans and settlers alike were originally rainwater deposits purified over the eons by seeping through numerous layers of soil to the sandstone bedrock. Underlying clay prevents the water from going any deeper and channels the flow from bedrock back to the valley surface. There is evidence that the springs were used at least 8,000 years ago.

In the old days (only a mere century ago) elk, golden eagles, prairie chickens, and wolves found a haven in what would later become the park. All these wild creatures have since disappeared from the scene, victims of agriculture and settlement. Yet today the park hosts red-tailed hawks, mink, and raccoons that have taken up residence along the Redwood River. At least 120 species of flowers bloom in and around the forest each year. Count the orange touch-me-nots and the yellow marsh marigolds.

While generally idyllic, the Camden area has seen its share of tragedy. John W. Lynd, the namesake of the village of Lynd (which is on the north side of the park), was the first white killed in the Dakota War of 1862. However, by 1868 the region had quieted and the town of Camden was growing. Even when the railroad went through neighboring Marshall, the community's gristmill kept its main street alive. By the 1930s the town had mostly faded into memory, its buildings shuttered and crumbling. Yet the Camden Woods remained a popular getaway spot for local picnickers. Historical markers point out the site of an American Fur Company trading post, a mill site and mill race, and the lookout point where settlers kept watch for bands of wandering Dakota. Poor Lynd must have been looking in the wrong direction.

The park has a regular series of programs that traces the history of the vicinity, as well as those focusing on plants, geology, and wildlife. A bulletin board near the information center (accessed off State Highway 23) relates times and dates between Labor Day and Memorial Day when the park is most used.

You may be interested in knowing of the Brawner Lake boat access near the Brawner Lake Wildlife Management Area just south of the park.

Where: The park is located off State Highway 23, 10 miles south of the Lyon County town of Marshall.

For more information: Camden State Park Manager, Route 1, Box 9, Lynd, MN 56157. Call 507-865-4530. Website: camden@starpoint.net.

Amenities: Unpack the roast chicken and spread your tablecloth at one of two picnic areas within the park. In case of rain each locale has a shelter. Bring the relatives. There are 140 tables available. A railroad track cuts through the park in a north-south direction. However it can be crossed in several locations via snowmobile and hiking trails. Just be very careful, especially on the far south crossing between the lower campgrounds and the primitive group camp.

The park offers 93 semimodern campsites (29 have electrical hookups). The group camp has space for 100 persons. There is a swimming pool, 10 miles of hiking trails, six miles of skiing trails, eight miles of snowmobile track, and three and four-fifths miles of bike-riding trails. There is even a mile of interpretive trail that is perfect for kids wanting to learn more about the woods.

Pets: Leashed or keep at home.

Activities: Interpretive programs, camping, cross-country skiing, horseback riding, snowmobiling, cycling.

Glacial Lakes State Park

To see some of the best examples of prime prairie land in Minnesota, stop at Glacial Lakes State Park. The preserve is located at the intersection of the west's original prairie and hardwood forests of the state's heart. While only one-tenth of one percent of Minnesota's original prairie land remains, the 1,880-acre park has an excellent variety of plants and animals indigenous to the native landscape. Prairie clover, pasque flowers, Indian grass, goldenrod, and other species dot the ground. The resident park interpreters can tell you the best times of year when the flowers blossom.

Glacial Hills is tucked into a geological phenomenon known as the Leaf Hills region of western Minnesota. A line of glacial hills, running some 10 to 19 miles, is unlike any other formation in the state. The band runs from Detroit Lakes southeasterly to Willmar. Geologists say that as glacial ice inched southward 10,000 years ago, it sliced off hills and bluffs. When the ice retreated it dumped the rocks, gravel, and dirt it had carried. The debris formed the undulating landscape stretching across west-central Minnesota. In the park there are several excellent examples of kames, the dome-shaped mounds formed when glacial refuse flowed down through holes in the ice. One is close to the picnic areas on the west side of spring-fed Mountain Lake, while at least four other major kames are along hiking trails to the south.

You can also see kettles, which are depressions in the ground formed when an ice block melts after being covered by debris. When the ice melted the ground cover collapsed to cause a hollow, which often became a lake or marsh. Two large kettles are found toward the central and south portions of the park, again reached by hiking trails. There are even several noticeable moraines, the leading edge of a glacier where a line of debris was dumped to form a ridge. Numerous erratics have been found in the park as well. These are boulders carried by the ice, having been picked up farther north during the glacial trip. Many of the rocks have ferrous oxide or iron ore, which indicates that they were carried from northeastern Minnesota or Canada. Other erratics are of granite or basalt, types of rock not commonly found in northwestern Minnesota.

Hike or ski about one and a half miles south on the marked trail into the maple forest to the park's highest elevation, some 1,352 feet above sea level. You can look out over the trees and imagine what it must have been like when those vast sheets of ice were crunching their ponderous way over the land.

Where: Glacial Lakes State Park is just five miles south of Starbuck, with an entrance from Pope County State Aid Highway 41.

For more information: Glacial Lakes State Park, 25022 County Road 41, Starbuck, MN 56381. Call 320-239-2860.

Amenities: The park has 39 campsites, four backpack sites, plus hot showers and modern toilets. There is a handicapped-accessible campground and beach. Nature trails, walk-in campsites, a group camping area, and a horseback-riding trailer park and camping round out the services. Canoe and rowboat rentals are available in the nearby town, and a boat-launching ramp is on Mountain Lake, the largest body of water within the park.

Pets: Leashed and tied.

Activities: Hiking, boating, camping, swimming, snowmobiling, cross-country skiing, horseback riding, and naturalist programs.

Lac qui Parle State Park

There is a sharp snap to the September air, as the month quickly moves into its third week. It is too early to sense the snow but any good Minnesotan can tell that winter is not far behind. There is a hiking trail, only about nine-tenths of a mile long that plays tag with the shoreline of Lac qui Parle lake. Stand there for a minute in the shadow of the trees and listen to the airline arrival and departure of the geese. Thousands of the birds honk and talk to each other as would a convention of debaters. Every bird has something to say . . . loudly. These fall flights continue until early December, with latecomers flapping away when the ice has already crusted the edges of the marsh. And when the birds return in the first half of March from their wintering grounds at Swan Lake, Missouri, it is grounds for another rejoicing.

Lac qui Parle State Park and its adjacent 27,000-acre wildlife management area have long been prime nesting sites for geese and other wildfowl, as well as waysides for pelicans and trumpeter swans. It is estimated that at least 400 goslings are born in the park each year, to take their place on the long flights to the south when the biological alarm clock rings. It was not always this way. Due to overhunting barely 100 geese were counted at Lac qui Parle as late as 1958. Today due to strict hunting controls (hunting is still allowed on 20,000 acres of the wildlife management area), the bird population has climbed again.

In addition to bird-watching fishing is another popular sport on the lake. However the state and the U.S. Corps of Engineers remind sportspeople that the area is a flood-control district, with a dam on the Minnesota River at the south end of the lake. Due to the fluctuating levels of the water, boaters have to be aware of reefs and submerged debris such as old logs. Anyone using the lake is encouraged to ask rangers in the visitors center about the condition of the day's water level before setting out. There is hardly anything worse than sitting in a sinking boat yards off-shore, especially when caution could have prevented a hazardous bottom-ripping snag.

The lake was formed following the Ice Age when glacial Lake Agassiz was drained to the south by what is called glacial River Warren. The torrent slashed out the Minnesota River valley. Eventually another opening came about in the north, forming the grandfather of today's Red River. Along the lengths of the ancient rivers, deltas formed where tributaries poured into the main flowage. The deltas formed natural dams, which resulted in such lakes as Lac qui Parle.

Ancient nomads hunted around the lake, followed centuries later by the Dakota, who called the body of water "the lake that talks." French traders gave the lake its current name. Around 1826, Joseph Renville, a man-about-the-woods and independent entrepreneur, built a stockade on the lakeshore. In 1835 missionaries established the first church in the state, built to bring Christianity to the Native Americans. The mission staff completed the first recorded grammar book and dictionary of the Dakota and set up a mill in which Minnesota's first cloth was woven. In the refurbished old mission, you can see the organ on which were played such lovely tunes as "The Dakota Hymn." The song also was known as "Many and Great, O God, Are Thy Things." About 40 contemporary Native American Congregational and Presbyterian churches in the Dakotas, Nebraska, and Montana can trace their roots to the Lac qui Parle mission.

Today after looking at the geese and other waterfowl, you can stop at the historical markers at the old fort and church site. They are found on the east side of the lake, along County Highway 32, just north of the intersection with State Highway 13. Regardless of the time of year, whether autumn or otherwise, pause at each memorial to mull over how rugged life must have been on Minnesota's frontier more than 100 years ago.

Where: The park is 12 miles northwest of Montevideo on the Minnesota River. You can get to the 530-acre site via Chippewa County Highway 13 and Lac qui Parle County

Highway 33. To the north and west of the park, is the 2,700-acre Lac qui Parle Wildlife Management Area.

For more information: Lac qui Parle State Park Manager, Route 5, Box 74A, Montevideo, MN 56265. Call 320-752-4736; Chippewa County Historical Society, Box 303, Montevideo, MN 56265. Call 320-269-7636.

Hours: The chapel is open from 8:00 A.M. to 8:00 P.M. daily from the last Sunday in April through Labor Day. You can tour the site at any time year-round.

Admission: Free to the mission historic site.

Amenities: The park offers 41 semimodern campsites, 21 of which have electricity. There are showers and flush toilets. A primitive group camp can accommodate 50 persons, and a horseback-riding camp can take up to 100 riders. The park has six miles of bridle paths, five miles of ski trails, and six miles of hiking trails. A trailer dump station is a welcome addition to the services there.

Pets: Leashed.

Best time to visit: At goose migration season in the spring and autumn.

Activities: Camping, hiking, skiing, horseback riding, and canoeing.

Lake Shetek State Park

Lake Shetek is the largest lake in southwestern Minnesota, spreading over 1,175 watery acres. The lake forms the head-waters of the Des Moines River. Although regularly stocked, the lake has been aerated since 1975, an ecological plus that has significantly increased the numbers of fish. So cast out for bullheads, walleye, northern pike, and other made-to-order-for-the-frying-pan fish. Inside the park is a state-managed pond for raising northern pike. The operation supplies pike for lakes throughout southwestern Minnesota.

In addition to fishing, bird-watching is a major recreational pursuit. Loon Island, hooked up to the mainland via a thin strip of land, is a bird sanctuary that offers plenty of chances to see nesting ducks. Hands off, of course. Leave the birds alone.

The park is located in the *Coteau des Prairies* region of the state, which translates to "slope of the prairies." At least four sheets of giant glacial ice crunched over the land from 1,100 to 2 million years ago. This flattened the land like a succession of massive rolling pins. The *Coteau* is formed by two moraines, ridges made up of geological junk dumped by retreating glaciers. Lake Shetek was made by one of them— the Altamont Moraine.

Although the park is surrounded by farmland, it is possible to think what the land might have been like prior to white settlement. The horizon would have been marked only by a few trees, unlike the woodlots and windbreaks planted by the farmers. For thousands of years early Native Americans had made the area their home. They lived near the small lakes that dotted the vicinity, hunted buffalo, and even farmed. European settlement put a different face on the land, confining the last Native American nation, the Dakota Sioux, to two small reservations on the Minnesota River.

Hungry and desperate, they were abandoned and ignored by the political system that placed them in the camps. Seeing that many of Minnesota's male population had left to fight the Civil War, the Dakota rose up. Tribal warriors killed 12 families near Lake Shetek and roamed the grasslands between the lake and New Ulm, 80 miles to the east. After the revolt was crushed, it was another two decades before any major settlement resulted. Yet life remained so tough that early pioneers were forced to sell buffalo bones for fertilizer.

Today you can get a sense of that history during interpretive programs in the park center. You can also take guided tours throughout the park to identify animals, plants, and geological formations. Several abandoned farm sites can be explored. But sometimes it is best to find a basswood tree, spread a blanket underneath, open a good book, and simply relax.

Where: The park is in Murray County only 14 miles northeast of Slayton and 33 miles southeast of Marshall. Entrance to the park is on County Highway 38, north of Currie.

For more information: Lake Shetek State Park Manager, 163 State Park Road, Currie, MN 56123-1018. Call 507-763-3256.

Amenities: There are 88 semimodern campsites, 68 with electricity. There are 20 rustic sites and a primitive camp for groups (accommodating up to 50 persons). A picnic area in the park serves 114 persons.

Pets: Leashed.

Best time to visit: Year-round.

Activities: Hiking, snowmobiling, skiing, fishing, boating, camping, loafing, photography, bird-watching, eating, and unwinding.

Pipestone National Monument/ Split Rock Creek Recreation Area

In 1836 frontier artist George Catlin related a tale of Minnesota's red pipestone and its origin. According to Sioux legend, said the observant chronicler, Great Spirit came to earth in the shape of a bird and alighted on a wall of rock (at the Pipestone quarries). He told all the tribes to gather around him. According to Catlin's narrative, Spirit then broke off a chunk of the red stone on which he was perched and formed it into a pipe. Smoking from the pipe, he told his "red children that this red stone was their flesh." The people were to smoke through it in homage to him, they must use the stone only for pipes, and it belonged to all tribes. Catlin said that the Native Americans subsequently considered the quarry ground as sacred territory and that no weapons were to be used there or brought on it.

Accounts of why the rock took on a sacred character differ from tribe to tribe, depending on the proximity to the quarries. One thing is certain, however, that the original people of North America were using pipes for at least 2,000 years before white settlement. Digging in the Minnesota quarry probably began in the 1600s, when metal tools acquired from European traders began to be used by various nations in the region. By 1700 the Dakota Nation controlled the quarries and bartered for other goods with the stone. Pipes eventually became a primary income source for carvers, and the Yankton Sioux secured unrestricted access to the quarries in an 1858 treaty. However, Anglo outsiders began digging pits and complaining about the Indian monopoly on the stone. In 1928, the tribe, which had been resettled on a reservation 150 miles away from the quarry, sold its interest in the site to the federal government. But when the area became a national monument in 1937, quarrying was again limited to Native Americans. You can see Indian carvers at work in the modern visitors center. The craft sales area in the same building is operated by the Pipestone Indian Shrine Association, with walls lined with intricately carved pipes. Each bears the name of its maker. The stems are made from native sumac or from such exotic material as redwood. Turtle totems, said to ensure fertility and long life, and other special objects are also available for purchase.

Yet by getting out of the building and walking along the paths that connect the quarry pits, you will gain a subtle sense of spirituality and history, if you allow yourself to be receptive to the feeling. The soft whisper of a breeze through the tall prairie grasses, the helloing chirp of a bobwhite, and the faint hum of a bee create a soothing sound track. Remember the admonition "to take nothing but pictures and leave nothing but tracks."

Since this region was originally a seabed, today's pipestone was once muddy clay that was covered with sand eons ago. Pressure and heat, along with a chemical reaction, formed the sand into quartzite, and the clay eventually became pipestone. Ask a craft worker in the visitors center if you can hold a piece of pipestone (leave the rock undisturbed when outside). You'll be fascinated by its smooth, soapy feel, knowing that the stone is very hard. But it is able to be carved into intricate shapes depicting animals and people at work, as well as geometric figures.

Climb along the well-marked path and pass such formations as Leaping Rock and the facelike Oracle, the racing flowage of Winnewissa Falls, and deep pits that have been quarried by the same Native American families for more than a century.

South of Pipestone is the Split Rock Creek Recreation Area, which became a 238-acre state park in 1938. Prior to its induction into the system, the neighborhood was treeless, typical of the vast expanse of open prairie that greeted the first settlers. A dam constructed on the creek in 1938 changed the face of the landscape, softening its visage with elm and ash shade trees. However there is still a remnant of the ancient prairie along the west side of the road on the way to the camping site. Park in the lot there and walk on the hillside where no plow has ever turned the soil. The variety of plant life in this relatively small plot is amazing, considering what was once hundreds of thousands of acres of undisturbed wilderness life. Mayflower, blazing star, and prairie smoke are only a few examples of plants you can easily identify. If the opportunity arises, try to visit several times throughout the year, because the panorama changes almost weekly.

Since the lake is the only large body of water in the county, numerous species of waterfowl flock to its shores. In the autumn, you can spot migrating Canada geese, pelicans, various types of ducks, and even swans. A fishing pier is located on the southwest shore of the lake, accessed through a picnic site, just before reaching the dam. Crappies, bass, and northern pikes usually rise quickly to your bait. It is your job to pull them into your creel.

Where: The visitors center is located on the north side of Pipestone. Look for signage along U.S. Route 75 and State Highways 23 and 30. If you are in Pipestone's downtown, drive north on Hiawatha Avenue, turn west at the "Song of Hiawatha" pageant grounds, drive past the Three Sisters stone landmark, and follow the road around a bend to the monument entrance. Split Rock Creek is six miles south of Pipestone on State Highway 23. Access to the recreation area is via Pipestone County Highway 20.

For more information: Pipestone National Monument and Indian Shrine Association, 36 Reservation Avenue, Pipestone, MN 56164-1269. Call 507-825-5464; Split Rock Creek Recreation Area Park Manager, Route 2, Jasper, MN 56144. Call 507-348-7908.

Hours: The Pipestone National Monument and the Indian Shrine Association are open from 8:00 A.M. to 6:00 P.M., Monday through Thursday and 8:00 A.M. to 8:00 P.M., Friday, Saturday, and Sunday, May 31 through Labor Day. Nonsummer hours are 8:00 A.M. to 5:00 P.M., daily.

Admission: $2.00 per adult or $4.00 per family to the monument. Free for Native Americans and children 16 and under. Seniors can purchase a Golden Age Card for $10.00 good for a lifetime of admissions to national parks.

Pets: No.

Best time to visit: Spring, summer, and fall.

Activities: Learn about Native American crafts and culture, tour the ancient quarries, enjoy bird-watching and flower identification.

6

Southeast

Now this is my kind of country: rolling hills shrouded with morning fog as thick as summer soup; rivers flush with fish; villages with German, Scandinavian, and Native American names; red barns; and blue silos. It's a world for bikers and canoers, fly fishermen and hikers, antiques crawlers and bargain hunters.

This section of Minnesota, where it nuzzles up against the Mississippi River and northern border with Iowa, was once covered by a vast hardwood forest. Millions of acres of oak, maple, basswood, ironwood, and cherry flowed over the ridges in a green wave. The trees marched westward to the grasslands where they petered out, eventually losing the fight to windswept prairie fires. It didn't take long for the settlers to clear the land. Within several generations even the stumps were gone. Farmland thick with corn, timothy, and oats replaced the forest. Bluffs eroded by tens of thousands of years of wind, rain, and snow make for a bumpy landscape as viewed from the air. From the ground pedaling along any of the country roads, there are thighstretching sections that seem to go on forever. It is lucky they don't. The sweeping rush downhill on the next lap is always exhilarating.

The Root River State Trail is among the best in the state, offering 28½ miles between Rushford and Fountain. The trail is a mere 120 miles southeast of the Twin Cities. It cuts through the hill country with its towering limestone facings, following the serpentine river most of the way. Look for wild turkeys and deer. The trail moves through historical Lanesboro, Peterson, and Whalan. There are bed-and-breakfasts, as well as inns and motels, for other levels of accommodations. Campgrounds are near Houston, Preston, and Lanesboro, as well as at Forestville/Mystery Cave and Beaver Creek Valley State Parks. Of course if you would rather canoe the route, the Root River presents 74 miles of pleasant paddling.

Cannon Valley Trail is another southeastern Minnesota winner, offering 19 miles of smooth pavement along the banks of the Cannon River. The trail is also used for hiking, biking, and cross-country skiing. Canoeing the Cannon is also a popular pastime.

This is trout country, especially around Caledonia, where fresh, cool streams tiptoe over their rocky beds in a gurgling symphonic tension. Bring your horsetail flies, hand-tied in Maine or New Brunswick, for the best rise out of these wily game fish. For a slower afternoon, sit by the heavier backwaters, where mud thick as sin moves around in the eddies. Fat bullheads wallow out of sight. Bring a can of angleworms and a cane pole. Plop down on the grassy bank and toss in a baited line. Sit, dream, and reflect on summer's sun. A mess of bullheads, fried up in beer batter, accompanied by fresh sweet corn and a pitcher of lemonade can be better than dinner at the Ritz.

Minnesota is the birthplace of the Mississippi River, which shows its growing strength along this rim of the state. Autumn is the best time for driving along the Great River

Road (State Highway 26 and U.S. Route 61). Trees become a thesaurus of shades: ochre, saffron, blaze, crimson. An end-of-year nip in the air is a perfect elixir. Roadside stands dot the countryside, laying out their cornucopia of squash, pumpkins, Indian corn, and apples. Ah, apples. Orchards march up and down the hills with the precision of a military brigade. In the heart of all this is La Crescent, which has earned the reputation as the Apple Capital of Minnesota. All along the highway bushels of Wealthies and Jonathans are overflowing the stalls. These are the perfect pick-me-up munch for a bike expedition.

Winona fronts the Mississippi, dangling its historic toes in the fast current. Winter's bald eagles soar over the ice-crusted inlets, looking for fish. Their widespread wings carry them high overhead, taking them from air current to air current, before they dive-bomb toward the river and lunch. An eagle observation deck is on the downtown riverwalk, quickly accessible from the main street and its shops.

The river affects all life along here, regardless of the season. Backwater inlets are home to herons, geese, and ducks. The Mississippi is the nation's flyway during migration time, when the skies darken with birds. In the secret, low-lying places, beaver, mink, and muskrat construct riverfront condos that are the envy of human developers who would die for those locations.

The hills above the Mississippi are deer heaven. They are so abundant in some places that motorists need to be doubly alert at night. A deer can bound across the dark country roads when least expected, causing fright and potential accidents.

Visitors can rent houseboats and motorboats for more water action. The Mississippi widens at Lake Pepin, creating a popular recreation site for water-skiers and powerboaters. Or if they want to stay landward, they can perch on a bluff and watch the *Delta Queen* rumble out of the past and into the summertime present. Its paddlewheels flashing, the steamboat's majesty is unrivaled on the river.

So regardless of the adventure—whether it's on land or water—this corner of the state has it all for outdoors lovers.

Bear Lake Wetlands

This combination of marsh and lake is a great place to spot ruddy ducks, grebes, and related waterbirds. The 1,600-acre site is eight miles south of Albert Lea and about one and a half miles west of U.S. Route 69. It is hard to imagine the extent of wild critters having their homes just out of sight of the rushing traffic. The best viewing is from late April through September. Visitors are asked not to disturb the nests, because the temperamental birds are especially vulnerable in late May and early June when hatchings occur. Watch, enjoy, and leave alone.

Where: Accessible by canoe on the north side of the lake on Freeborn County Highway 9.
For more information: The Rice Lake State Park office, which houses the state's Department of Natural Resources wildlife manager, can provide information on the Bear Lake Wetlands. Rice Lake State Park, 8485 Rose Street, Owatonna, MN 55060. Call 507-455-5841.

Beaver Creek Valley State Park

The soft sighing of cottonwoods along Beaver Creek is a symphony, especially on a lazy summer afternoon. The dull drone of cicadas, the rat-a-tat-tat of a hungry woodpecker whacking at a stump, and the gurgle of creek water over the black stones make real music. Even the fly casting of a hip-booted angler upstream is part of the gentleness of the day. Gracefully dipping, the rod flips the filament line and fly through the sun-touched haze where it delicately plops into a deep pool. What looks like a trophy brown trout rises in a flash of sparkling water. Caught! The fisherman has another prize, but he bends over for the obligatory sportsmanlike release, thus ensuring a steady supply of trout for subsequent casts.

Beaver Creek bubbles out of a spring that remains active even through the winter, allowing the furry denizens of the woods plenty of liquid refreshment. And in the summer the gurgle of clear water ensures that Minnesota's renowned mosquitoes have a hard time roosting and then pricking campers. In autumn the walnut, oak, maple, and basswood explode in fiery colors. Of course spring is the time for viewing jack-in-the-pulpit and trillium, as well as the secretive morel mushroom. Regardless of the season the park has plenty of *au naturel*ness to go around. A small park, only 650 acres, it attracts about 48,000 to 50,000 visitors per year, ranking it 42nd out of the 62 state parks in visitor use.

The landscape is rugged, as part of the "driftless" area of Minnesota untouched eons ago by galloping glaciers. Melting ice runoff swelled streams and rivers that subsequently cut through the limestone as easily as a sharp knife cuts through cream cheese. In some places the valley walls are as high as 250 feet above the creek bed, allowing geology fans to clearly observe the various layers of sandstone and dolomite. The creek tumbles over rocks and stones in a swift rush to the Root River, where the common waters flow on to the Mississippi River, along the Minnesota–Iowa border near Brownsville.

Since the land is so rugged, little of it was able to be farmed when the settlers came into the area in the 1850s. While they cleared land for pastures, much of the original growth remains. The park, in fact, is home to numerous rare species of plants that are no longer found anywhere else in Minnesota. The Minnesota County Biological Survey has counted at least 86 new rare plant locations in and around the park, augmenting the 102 significant examples of natural community types, such as white pine, oak-dotted savannas, bluff prairies, seepage fern, and maple and basswood forests. Among the endangered species of plant life finding a haven in Beaver Creek, are the sweet-scented Indian plantain, wild indigo, rough-seeded fameflower, and the heart-leaved skullcap. Even some golden saxifrage is present within the park, a relic of plant life present during the Ice Age, according to botanists. Serious nature lovers may wish to pick up a report on Houston County's rare plant species, available free at the park office.

With all this hard-to-find-elsewhere vegetation, it is only proper that unusual animal species can also be found in Beaver Creek. Prairie voles, sandhill cranes, bullfrogs, and numerous snake varieties can be spotted. Since all are protected, observant hikers are asked to report sightings to the park ranger. This is true even when seeing a timber rattler. Look but certainly don't touch when confronted by the shy snake. They are grumpy (read "dangerous") when aroused. Naturally there are also several busy beavers at work in their namesake park. The furry flat-tailers can sometimes be spotted along the creek at the north end of the park.

When Anne Selness was park ranger at Beaver Creek, she inventoried rare butterflies in the park. Before she moved on to work in other parks, she had counted more than 50 species there. Selness was well qualified to poke around the place, having camped and hiked there as a youngster. In fact, her grandfather, George Hendel, used to have pastureland in the area and her dad, Howard Hendel, still owns some property within the park boundaries. The first official butterfly count was held in 1995, organized by the Xerces Society, a national organization of butterfly-watchers. At the park Selness held training sessions for amateur first-time counters, some as young as 12 years old. She now is community education director for the Caledonia Independent School District.

Eight miles of trails range through the park, taking campers and hikers to the creek, ridges, wooded lots, and open spaces. None are easily accessible to the physically challenged because of the rolling land formations. However several of the campsites are geared to folks who need special picnic tables under which their wheelchairs can fit. These sites are closest to the sanitation stations for easy use.

Where: The park is five miles west of Caledonia on Houston County Highway 1, off State Highway 76.
For more information: Beaver Creek Valley State Park Manager, Route 2, Box 57, Caledonia, MN 55921. Call 507-724-2107.
Amenities: Beaver Creek Valley State Park has 42 semimodern campsites, a trailer dump station, showers, and toilets. There are also six walk-ins. The primitive group camp accommodates 100 persons. There are seven and a half miles of hiking trails and four miles of cross-country ski trails. The park is open year-round, but the gates are closed from 10:00 P.M. to 8:00 A.M. except for registered campers.
Other: Native Americans once roamed the area, and archaeologists have found stone tools in the park. Homesteaders eventually lived along the valley, and there are the remains of a settler's cabin in the park.

Forestville/Mystery Cave State Park

Forestville offers a generous dollop of history, geology, and recreational possibilities, making it a favorite southeastern Minnesota getaway. It has one of the best trout-fishing streams in the state, with crafty browns seemingly as gigantic as that *Jaws* shark character in its feeding frenzy. Of course you do have to catch and reel them in, which is always an art. Some of the fish get to be 16 inches in length, weighing up to two pounds each. For bait use worms, spinners, even flies. Yet there must be something in the genetic makeup of trout that makes fishermen have to guess what lure to use every time they cast. Four miles of great fishing along the Root River system are within the park, while you can also trek upstream some five miles and downstream 18 miles for more angling opportunities.

In addition to providing a plentiful supply of trout, the rushing waters in the park's streams are a plus for another reason: no mosquitoes. Every time you stroll along Sinkhole Ridge Trail, you should be soooooo glad that none of Minnesota's "state birds" are in the vicinity.

But speaking of birds, some 175 species have been observed at the park, including several varieties of the seldom-seen warblers. A good-sized contingent of wild turkeys has also found Forestville perfect for their gobbler gatherings. Along with the birds, patient hikers can sometimes spot a wily gray fox, as well as its more numerous red cousins. There is the usual collection of white-tailed deer, possums, raccoons, and mink. And rattlesnakes, warns Mark White, the friendly, outgoing park manager.

"Leave them alone," he said. "They are rare and protected by state law." Sightings, however, should be reported to the park office. White, who has been at the park since 1982, appreciates knowing where his slithery friends have been spotted.

Rattlers love the Forestville countryside as much as other outdoors enthusiasts. There are plenty of rocky bluffs on which they can sun, because the park is located in the Karst region of Minnesota. Karst (dissolved limestone) occurs in areas of such soluble rocks. Rainwater is made acidic as it bubbles through the soil and picks up carbon dioxide from the decay of organic matter. This type of water can subsequently dissolve rock—over thousands of years, of course. Subsequently the Forestville area abounds in sinkholes as a result of this geological reworking of the landscape. Mystery Cave, part of the park grounds, was caused by such water action. Other caves in the area were supposedly used during the Civil War to hide horses to avoid conscription by the U.S. Army. In the 1920s moonshiners and rumrunners reportedly used the caves to stash their illegal booze.

Untouched by the most recent glacial action (the last ice cube to crunch the countryside was some million years back), this driftless area has remained a maze of hills and 200-foot-high cliffs, which made it hard or impossible to farm. I've always been thankful for that, because today's forest visitors can enjoy the woods much as they were a hundred years ago. A thick carpet of sugar maple, hickory, aspen, oak, basswood, and black walnut covers the land. Several rare stands of white pine and tall-grass prairie are also located within the park environs.

"There is a lot of demand on the park's campgrounds since we are so close to the Root River bike trail. This park also has the highest use by horseback riders than any other park in the state," manager White pointed out. Riders love the 16 miles of horse trails over steep terrain in the park's quiet, tree-shaded interior. They are generally careful of the plant life when fording the streams. "Most folks are pretty good about taking care of the park grounds," White said thankfully.

With a maze of more than 12 miles of caverns, Mystery Cave is the longest in Minnesota. Talk about going underground and saving time! The South Branch of the Root River meanders five miles in a twisty-turning way topside, while part of its flowage disappears near the cave entrance and reappears one and a half miles away at Seven Springs, where it rejoins the river. Sometimes in the hot, dry summers, the entire stream sinks out of sight, filtering through the gravel and into crevices along the river bottom. Deep, dark—but not dangerous—Mystery Cave harbors four species of bats and plenty of odd geological formations. Be careful not to touch any of the walls, because your skin's natural oils can discolor the rock surface.

The cave was purchased in 1988 as an addition to Forestville State Park, with the main park entrance five and a half miles away.

In the center of the park is the historic town site of Forestville, founded in 1853 as a farming trade center in pre-railroad days. In 1858 the village had 100 residents, two general stores, a gristmill, a brickyard, two hotels, and a school, said Dennis Seglem, site manager. Seglem and his staff of interpreters work for the Minnesota Historical Society, which manages the property as a living-history center.

"For a short time, there was even an unofficial North Forestville and a South Forestville, separated by the road," he said. "It was rather like the Twin Cities, but Minneapolis–St. Paul grew and became successful. Forestville didn't." When the railroad chose another direction for its tracks, bypassing the village, the community soon began to wither and die.

The staff portrays the town as it would have appeared in the 1890s. There is a general store plus barns, outbuildings, and the office of Thomas Meighen, who owned most of the surrounding property. Dina Julson acts out the role of Martha, Meighen's sister, and other trained interpreters have similar characters to portray.

While now only seen as a reenactment, the real-life family's connection with the park started as early as 1903, when

Meighen suggested making his lands a state park. But there was little support or encouragement for his plan because of the lack of available state funding. Political foot-dragging led to other delays.

"It is unique to have such buildings, thousands of artifacts from that era, the surrounding parkland, and all the outdoors recreational opportunities in one area," said Seglem. To preserve the rustic, quiet character of the crossroads community, autos must park in a lot about an eighth of a mile away. You then cross a bridge over a small river and walk into town, where it is easy to turn one's mind back to another era.

"Rainy days in the park ensure our busiest times here," Seglem laughed. "It's a fantastic place to bring the family for a few hours when everything outside is dripping wet."

Where: Forestville/Mystery Cave State Park is tucked into Fillmore County halfway between Preston and Spring Valley. The entrance to the park is four miles south of State Highway 16 on Fillmore County Highway 5 and two miles east on Fillmore County Highway 12. The best routes to the cave are east on County Highway 16 off U.S. Route 63 or south off County Highway 5 from State Highway 16.

For more information: Forestville/Mystery Cave Park Office, Route 2, Box 128, Preston, MN 55965. Call 507-352-5111 (park) or 507-937-3251 (Mystery Cave).

Admission: Tour fees are $7.00 for adults and $4.00 for ages 5 to 12. Youngsters under four are $1.00.

Amenities: There seems to be something recreation-wise for everybody nearby, ranging from public boat-launch sites along the Mississippi River to 43 campgrounds, five beaches, and 45 individual picnic sites in the vicinity. For winter lovers there are 1,200 miles of snowmobile trails within 50 miles of the park. The longest are the Mower County Trail (182 miles) and the Gopherland Trail in Houston County (160 miles). Tours of the cave are offered daily between Memorial Day and Labor Day. A lighted, one-hour historic tour winds along ramped concrete walkways and is readily accessible. A two-hour Minnesota Caverns Tour is offered only on weekends and is not recommended for little kids with short legs or folks with heart conditions. Physically-challenged persons should be aware that the two-hour tour involves a great deal of walking along gravel paths. Handheld electric lanterns are the only light source.

Best time to visit: Year-round.

Activities: Hiking, camping, fishing, bird-watching, cross-country skiing, picnicking, horseback riding, touring historical sites.

Other: The park was founded in 1963, with most of the boundaries established by 1969. Administrative control of the village of Forestville was given to the Minnesota Historical Society in 1977. For bikers the muscle-stretching terrain around Forestville is unparalleled. The Root River State Trail, located between Fountain and Rushford, extends 35 miles along an abandoned railroad grade. The path wends its way through the valley, with plans to eventually link it to the town of Preston (which calls itself the trout-fishing capital of the region) and the park itself.

Hay Creek Management Area, Richard J. Dorer Memorial State Forest

Hay Creek was one of the first blocks of land purchased in 1961 to form this state forest. It is located two miles south of Red Wing in northern Goodhue County, via State Highway

58. Currently the Hay Creek region is 1,500 acres of rugged hills carpeted with dense groves of black cherry, oak, elm, birch, and basswood. The creek is lined with cottonwoods, willow, soft maple, and ash. All this timber makes Hay Creek a valuable component of the state forest, where timber sales have helped boost the local economy. Most planting sites were old farm fields that were marginal to begin with, so the reforestation of these lands has been doubly beneficial. The production of wood demonstrates how the careful management of resources pays off economically, environmentally, and scenically.

An eight-mile marked and groomed trail system roller coasters from creek bottom to ridgelines. Hikers and horseback riders enjoy the summertime (foot folks, watch where you step!), and snowmobilers are allowed use of the system in the winter.

Where: State Highway 58 bisects the park, making it easy to reach for the folks who live in Red Wing, about two miles north of the management unit. Signage along the highway indicates the exit points to parking lots, with the lot on the south end of the unit near a picnic area. Hiking trails angle out from both.

For more information: Area Forest Supervisor, Box 69, Lake City, MN 55041. Call 612-345-3216.

Lake Louise State Park

A flight of Canada geese twirled overhead, framed against the gray, rain-touched afternoon sky in a ballet of feathers. Their honking sounded as if a clutch of poker-playing widows was arguing over who had the ace of spades in a heated hand of five-card stud. They zoomed above the pin

maples in a ragged formation, each bird with
its wings and neck outstretched in a
feathered т.
     A thicket alongside the shallow
lake, just behind a narrow bridge that
led from the mainland to a small island,
made perfect cover for us. We watched as the geese cir-
cled once, twice, then three times before settling into the
muddy water with a flurry. Splashing and calling to each
other, they set about their business of primping, eating, and
resting up for the next leg of their annual spring migration
northward. After an appropriate amount of razzing each other
and filling stomachs, the flock again gathered momentum
with a great flapping of wings and lifted off to the north.
     It was just in time, as the rain's sprinkles turned into a
steady drizzle, thereby softening the late-May evening. Steam
rose from the newly planted cornfields that surrounded the
park, and stalks of wildflowers bent under the rain. Somewhere out in the park was a colony of the rare *Allium cernuum*,
a nodding wild onion. Lake Louise State Park is one of the
few identified sites in the state where the endangered onion
species has been found. Several researchers for the Minnesota
Heritage Program stumbled across this valuable find on a field
trip in 1982. But on a recent visit, no sight of the onions was
obvious, at least to the untrained eye.
     Lake Louise is an oasis amid the rich farming country of
southeastern Minnesota. Dozens of bird species make the area
a watcher's paradise, attracted to the mixed habitat of hardwoods and abandoned pastureland and fields that make up the
park. A prime stop on the migration routes for many birds,
such as the geese, Lake Louise comprises 1,168 acres. White-
tailed deer, foxes, raccoons, and other wildlife share the woodlands. The park contains two spring-fed streams that join

inside the park environs to form the Upper Iowa River. In the late 1800s a dam and gristmill were located there.

The park is one of Minnesota's oldest recreational areas. The area was surveyed in 1853, and the town of Le Roy was mapped out. Subsequently the river was dammed. Shortly afterward, however, the railroad came through from the east, bypassing the original town site. This necessitated a move southward to the current location, so local businesses would be closer to the railroad's transportation potential. The gristmill was abandoned, and the Hambrecht family, who owned land by the mill pond, donated three acres to the village to be used for recreation. The site was then known as Wildwood Park, with the mill pond called Lake Louise after one of the Hambrecht-family youngsters. In 1962 Le Roy donated Wildwood Park to the state, which then expanded its original 70 acres to today's size.

Motorboats are a no-no on the lake, but canoes and rowboats are permitted. The park offers 11.6 miles of hiking trails, 9.7 miles of horse trails, 2.2 miles of cross-country ski trails, and 9.3 miles of snowmobile trails. There is a mile-long interpretive trail as well. A trailer at the park entrance doubles as an office for the resident ranger.

Where: Lake Louise State Park is located barely a sneeze away over the Minnesota–Iowa border in Mower County. It is 1½ miles north of the small town of Le Roy on County Highway 14. To get there exit west on State Highway 56 from the north-south U.S. Route 63, one of the main roadways linking both states. Signs in the town indicate directions to the park. Motorists can also exit south from I-90 onto State Highway 56, about a 28-mile ride to the park entrance.

For more information: Lake Louise State Park, Route 1, Box 184, Le Roy, MN 55951. Call 507-324-5249.

Hours: The park is closed, except to registered campers, from 10:00 P.M. until 8:00 A.M. the following day. Loud noises are prohibited after 10:00 P.M.

Amenities: The park has an open-sided picnic shelter and 22 campsites, 11 of which have electricity. A primitive group camp can accommodate 100 persons, with a nearby horse campground for 50 riders (keep horses in the tie-up area, not near the campgrounds, say several prominently placed signs). There is a trailer dump station. A small museum, honoring the Hambrechts, is also on the grounds. However the frame building, with antique farm implements and other artifacts, is only open weekdays in the summer. Old Wildwood Days Celebration is held in the park early each June, with interpretive walks, birding, and other outdoor activities.

Pets: All must be leashed. They are not allowed in park buildings.

Best time to visit: Year-round.

Activities: Hiking, camping, fishing, bird-watching, cross-country skiing, picnicking, reunions and family gatherings, horseback riding, canoeing, and boating. Motor bikes and other licensed vehicles are allowed only on designated roads, not on trails.

Other: The park is located along the Upper Iowa River, a watershed that extends from Minnesota into Iowa. Canoe perfect, the shallow river eddies through farmland and past small bluffs on its way to link with the Iowa River and the north branch of the Turkey River. There are numerous in points along the waterway for paddlers. The vicinity of the state park was barely touched by the Ice Age. Subsequently limestone bedrock is fairly close to the surface and topped by only a thin layer of glacial remains. In some places within the park, this underlying limestone has been washed away, forming a sinkhole. Aside from these depressions, the park is level. This makes it easy for beginning cross-country skiers and amateur horseback riders.

Lamprey Pass Wildlife Management Area

If blue herons and egrets are on your bird-watching sheet, or if beavers, white-tailed deer, and raccoons are on the fauna list, make a pit stop at Lamprey Pass. This 1,300-acre management zone includes Mud and Howard Lakes, plus several ponds and scattered woodlots. The prime viewing times for birds are April through August. Watch for posted areas that are closed to the public when herons are nesting in the spring.

Where: Located one mile south of Forest Lake, about a mile west of I-35. Exit County Highway 23/State Highway 97 from the interstate. Then take the first access road that parallels the highway. Go beyond the park-and-ride lot to the Department of Natural Resources parking area. Walk past the metal gate to enter the woods.

For more information: Carlos Avery Wildlife Management Area, 5463 West Broadway, Forest Lake, MN 55025. Call 651-296-5290.

Nerstrand–Big Woods State Park

The Big Woods. *Bois Grande.* Images of creepy, crawly things that go bump in the night, where Hansel and Gretel became lost, where hobbits are afraid to roam. But dispel all fairy-tale images from your mind. The Nerstrand–Big Woods State Park is sundappled, dazzling, and delightful regardless of the season. The park is almost all that remains of two million acres of timber that covered central Minnesota when the first settlers arrived in 1854. The Cannon and Minnesota Rivers on the south had protected the region from prairie fires, allowing the trees to grow in a broad belt between what is now Faribault on the east, Mankato on the south, and St. Cloud on the north.

Axes were something else however. The newcomers set up small woodlots within the forest, hacking out five- and 10-acre parcels at a time. During the 1930s heavy-duty logging cleared hundreds of acres at a time. By the 1940s a few environmentalists realized that there soon would not be any big woods remaining if conditions continued. Subsequently a plan was developed with the State Department of Conservation and the U.S. Forest Service to acquire what remained. By 1945 about 1,280 acres were acquired, and the Nerstrand Woods was established by the Minnesota legislature.

A major anniversary party was held at the park in 1995, celebrating the Big Woods's 50th anniversary. "We had auto tours around the park perimeter, special hikes, and school programs," recalled area naturalist Elaine Feikema. "People were amazed at the closed canopy of branches over the narrow roads and the variety of plant and animal life," she said.

The Nerstrand–Big Woods is rich in biological diversity, as the scholars would say. So it is double fun to spot green-backed herons, blue-winged teal, American woodcock, and dozens of other bird varieties, as well as numerous species of wildflowers. We've enjoyed hiking there almost any time of year, but May is always the best as the warm ground opens up to all sorts of life forms in the great food web. Spiders set up elaborate, dew-catching nets amid the dried stalks of last year's grasses. A red-backed vole scurries through the leaves on some mission . . . probably to do with lunch. Pileated woodpeckers hammer hard at ancient tree trunks, seeking out the tastiest sowbugs and carpenter ants.

No insects for me, however, even though roaming the woods is a delight. I prefer to drive over to Nerstrand Catering and Butcher Shop in the nearby town with its 210 lucky residents. The folks there have access to the best hot dogs, seasoned sausages, and ring baloney this side of Germany. The catering service has accommodated shindigs in the Twin Cities (once even serving Monster Pecs Man Arnold S. when he came to a friend's wedding in Minneapolis). Around noon the shop usually serves up rib-eye-steak sandwiches, sloppy joes, or some other delight for area farmers, shopkeepers, and teachers who know the precise time when to drop by for a munch. Or you can put together some wild-beef sticks, Danish Havarti cheese, black bread, fruit juice, and carrot sticks and head back for a picnic in the Big Woods. Beats chewing on larvae.

The Nerstrand school district is actively involved in keeping the park tidy, using the Big Woods as a ready laboratory. So don't be alarmed if a gaggle of kids bursts out of the oaks while you are on a reflective stroll. They are busy hunting "good stuff" for lab projects. "We work very closely with the schools in the area. They realize what a fantastic natural, educational resource the woods offers," said naturalist Feikema.

Where: From the north the park is located 11 miles from Northfield (site of the famed James Gang bank raid in 1876). Take State Highway 264 southeast out of town and follow the signs. From the south, take County Highway 20 northeast from State Highway 60 east out of Faribault. Turn right on County Highway 27 at Cannon City to Nerstrand, and follow the signs to the park. The jaunt from that direction is 12 miles from Nerstrand.

For more information: Nerstrand–Big Woods State Park Manager, 9700 170th Street East, Nerstrand, MN 55053. Call 507-334-8848.

Hours: The park is open year-round, but on a daily basis the gates are closed from 10:00 P.M. to 8:00 A.M., except for registered campers.

Amenities: The park has 54 semimodern campsites, 28 of which have electrical hookups. There are showers, flush toilets, picnic tables, and fire rings. In addition there are

13 rustic sites and a group camp for 200 persons. Meander the 14 miles of hiking trails, ski the eight miles of cross-country trails, or snowmobile the five miles of trails.

Pets: Leashed.

Best time to visit: Open year-round. In early spring the trillium, Dutchman's-breeches, wild ginger, and marsh marigolds explode in color. The seasons then move into a symphony of violets, lady's slippers, and wild parsnips. But beware the sneezeweed in August. For ease in tracking the flora, pick up a wildflower checklist in the park office near the main gate.

Activities: Camping, hiking, bird-watching.

Other: For great eats contact Nerstrand Catering, Nerstrand, MN 55053. Call 507-334-8848.

Great River Bluffs State Park (formerly O.L. Kipp State Park)

This is a favorite park because of the scenic views overlooking the Mississippi River. Easy walking trails take visitors along the bluffs for a reflective getaway. Benches, rock formations, and grassy spaces under trees provide sit-down opportunities for weary feet and souls. The park has excellent stands of oak and hickory, with some pine plantations for a more formal look. There is even a native stand of white cedar, a rare and appreciated sight. A scattering of prairie sites is home to red-winged blackbirds and other birds. Some parts of the park are nicknamed "goat prairies" because of the 40- and 50-degree slopes, so steep that only goats could graze on them, according to old-time settlers. These 20 or so patches of prairie face south, receiving plenty of rich sunshine.

The park was originally named after Orrin Lansing Kipp, who had been with the Minnesota Department of Highways for more than 50 years, retiring as an assistant commissioner in the mid-1950s. He helped develop the state's trunk road system. These roads—such as Apple Blossom Drive, which leads to the park entrance—meander through some of Minnesota's most scenic landscapes.

The park was authorized by the Minnesota legislature in 1963 and the land was finally secured in the 1970s. It officially opened in the 1976–77 season. The name was changed to Great River Bluffs State Park in 1977. According to the park rangers, the new name gives visitors more of a sense of what the park has to offer. Kipp would be proud of how Minnesotans and other outdoor lovers have taken the 3,000-acre site to their hearts. The park, in a "driftless" area untouched by glaciers, was created within the Richard J. Dorer Memorial Forest. While the last glaciers bypassed this region, they left an imprint. By taking any of the trails through Great River Bluffs State Park, a hiker can spot areas where the erosion of the raging Mississippi River gouged out the rock. Glacial melt swelled the river, adding enough muscle for it to carve through hundreds of feet of limestone. Visitors are warned to stay on the paths so they don't disturb the loess. This is the wind-blown dust deposited after the glaciers left the surrounding areas, forming much of the rich earth on the park's steep ridges. The loess is easily eroded, which causes uncounted environmental problems if disturbed. The site is designated as a "natural state park," which means the restoration and protection of natural resources are the prime mission of the staff. It should also be the goal of anyone visiting as well.

Since the Richard J. Dorer Memorial State Forest was mentioned, hikers in the know enjoy the forest's six-and-a-half mile Plowline Trail with its south and north loops. The path rises and falls on the swells of the land, provides easy walking in the summer, but it is moderate to difficult when cross-country skiing. The hardwood forest, established in 1961, was named for Dorer, a local environmentalist who lobbied to secure land for the preserve with its valuable black-walnut and white-pine stands. Some of the best hiking is along two spurs off the north loop of the Plowline, which extend out to overlooks of the Stockton and Mississippi River valleys. They are great for viewing grim turkey vultures soaring over the treeline and watching finches dart in a staccato of yellow and black through the branches.

In case there are any questions, Leon Bronk was the landowner from whom the property was purchased in 1969. The management area is 761 acres in size, overlooking valleys some 500 feet below. The scenic looks are unrivaled anywhere in Minnesota's bluff country.

Where: The park is located 20 miles southeast of Winona at the junction of U.S Route 61 and I-90. Exit at Winona County Highway 12 off I-90 and take Apple Blossom Drive (County Highway 3) to the park entrance. To get to the Plowline Trail, which is in what is called the Leon Bronk Management Unit of the Richard J. Dorer Memorial State Forest, take U.S. Route 14 west from Winona to Winona County Highway 23. Drive north two and one-tenths miles to Hillsdale Township Road Number 6. Go east on Number 6 for a half mile to the lower parking lot of the Leon Bronk Management Unit. Then walk up the hill for about a mile to the upper parking lot and cross around the gate. Walk some 175 feet, and the Plowline Trail south loop is on the right.

For more information: Great River Bluffs State Park Manager, Route 4, Winona, MN 55987. Call 507-643-6849.

Hours: The park is closed, except to registered campers, from 10:00 P.M. until 8:00 A.M. the following day. Loud noises are prohibited after 10:00 P.M.

Amenities: Great River Bluffs State Park has a campground with 31 sites, each with picnic tables, fire ring, and proximity to modern toilets. The park's pioneer camp is available to Scouts, church groups, and others. There are 20 picnic tables scattered along the ridge above the Mississippi, each isolated from the others by trees and shrubs for a bit of woodland privacy.

Pets: All must be leashed. They are not allowed in park buildings.

Best time to visit: Year-round.

Activities: Hiking, camping, bird-watching, cross-country skiing, picnicking, writing poetry, loafing with a friend in the shade of a black walnut.

Rice Lake State Park

Seeing an ostrich in the Rice Lake State Park is not improbable, although unlikely. After all, one of the Midwest's largest ostrich farms is across the main frontage road from the park's front door. But none of the gangly Down Under birds have ever been spotted enjoying the lake environs from within, as have many of their feathered cousins including the pileated woodpecker. This particular woodpecker is the state's largest head-hammerer. The 1,000-acre park is a prime spot for bird-watchers from around southern Minnesota, northern Iowa, and as far away as Chicago.

Sightings have included the western grebe, blue-winged teal, northern oriole, caspian tern, great egret, yellow-throated vireo, and dozens more. Migrations in the spring and autumn bring in the likes of the palm warbler and the ring-necked duck. The juxtaposition of lake, woods, and prairie land results in excellent viewing opportunities. Minnesota's southernmost nesting place for loons has also been recorded as being at Rice Lake. There are three miles of hiking trails meandering through the meadows and woods, as well as along the rim of the lake. This ease of access on the north side of the four-foot-deep lake takes confirmed bird-watchers into most of the best areas. Permission from the park manager is necessary to visit the undeveloped south side of the lake, although a five-site primitive campground reached only by canoe is available on that shoreline.

"We manage the lake primarily for the bird population," points out park manager Roger Heimgartner. "It is a great rest area for migratory species," he points out. The lake is great for canoeing, being shaped in a shallow, spring-fed horseshoe, which means that there is constant protection from the wind. Heimgartner points out that the lake forms what is called a fire shadow on its eastern side. The water body broke up prairie fires as they raged up from the southwest in the early years. Subsequently the protected land behind the lake—in its "shadow"—could then accommodate and protect tree growth.

Five hundred million years ago, southeastern Minnesota was a shallow sea. Eventually over eons, the bottom sediment turned to rock that was hundreds of feet deep. Then along came years of glacial refrigeration that flattened the by then dry countryside. Rice Lake is the result of landscaping finalized approximately 400,000 years ago during the great Kansan Ice Age, the second of North America's four major bouts with mile-high ice. The first Ice Age, the Nebraskan, had done some preliminary shaping and dumping of refuse, but the Kansan added the last touches. The bullhead-packed lake is a depression left in a vast pile of rubble and drift abandoned when the Kansan ice melted away, sloping the land westward. A vast oak-dotted savanna evolved, as part of Minnesota's Southern Oak Barrens, which had covered about 7 percent of the state before the advent of white encroachment. This savanna formed a wide transition zone that linked the western prairies and the deciduous forest on the east. A few remaining burr oaks inside the park, which were spared by settlers' axes, are all that remain. The original lush prairie vegetation is also gone, except for a few remnants along railroad rights-of-way and in abandoned cemeteries, such as the one found on the eastern edge of the park.

Native Americans set up camps along the shore, harvesting the wild rice that grew there and hunting throughout the region. They kept coming back to Rice Lake, even after the Treaty of Mendota in 1851, which was to have forced them out of Minnesota and into the country to the west. Early settlers tell of using Indian trails running from Rice Lake to the Zumbro River to the southeast (near what is now Rochester). The lake is actually the headwaters of the river, its outlet forming the South Branch of its Middle Fork. White settlers tried to dam the lake's outlets, to provide energy to run a gristmill located in Wasioja to the east. This resulted in the depletion of the water, and the mill eventually had to close, burning to the ground in 1891.

The pioneers tried to establish a town near where the current lake exits, along the north boundary of the park along Dodge County Highway 20. But the community moved on to more prosperous areas when the railroads came through Minnesota farther to the south. All that remains of the town of Rice Lake is the Rice Lake Church, built in 1857.

Now only the gentle prairie winds ruffle the high grasses and bluebells of the park. On calm nights wild turkeys sometimes can be heard gobbling in the distance.

Where: Rice Lake State Park is seven miles east of Owatonna on Steele County Highway 19. Owatonna is 66 miles south of the Twin Cities on I-35.

For more information: Rice Lake State Park, 8485 Rose Street, Owatonna, MN 55060. Call 507-455-5871.

Hours: The park is closed, except to registered campers, from 10:00 P.M. until 8:00 A.M. the following day. Loud noises are prohibited after 10:00 P.M.

Amenities: In addition to the canoe campsites, the park has a semimodern camp with 42 sites and a primitive group camp accommodating 100 persons. The semimodern sites have picnic tables, fire ring, tent area, and parking space. Flush toilets, showers, and 16 electrical sites are nearby. Running water is supplied in the sanitation building. The primitive group area has a pit toilet and a hand pump for water, in addition to picnic tables, tent sites, and fire rings. There are three miles of easy cross-country ski trails and a two-and-a-half-mile snowmobile trail.

Pets: Leash 'em!

Best time to visit: Migration times in spring and fall for birdwatching; otherwise, all year long for other species.

Activities: Hiking, camping, fishing, bird-watching, crosscountry skiing. Motor bikes and other licensed vehicles are allowed only on designated roads, not on trails.

Other: Nearby Owatonna is a city of 20,000 residents, and home to several colleges, the usual round of golf courses, and quiet city parks. There is a renovated depot with steam engine No. 201, once driven by the famed Casey Jones of folk-song fame. The most well known of the city's landmarks is the Norwest Bank, originally the Farmer's Bank of Owatonna, designed by Louis Sullivan in 1907. The Village of Yesteryear, on the Steele County fairgrounds, consists of 10 buildings from the pioneer era.

Reno Bottoms Delta/Reno Management Unit, Richard J. Dorer Memorial State Forest

You take the low road. The flood basin-land plain forests and marshes of the Reno Bottoms Delta make up the Mississippi

River flood plain from Reno southward to the Iowa border. Most of the land is within the Upper Mississippi River Wildlife and Fish Refuge. The levee road leading from Reno to Lock and Dam No. 8 bypasses the edge of the refuge. White-oak trees dominate the bit of low-lying land amid the backwater bogs. Moor hens and sandhill cranes are numerous, seen hopscotching around the lily pads. On a summer night a bullfrog chorus can be thunderous.

And I'll take the high road. The Reno Management Unit (RMU) of the memorial forest is about 15 miles south of La Crescent, overlooking the Mississippi River and the tiny community of Reno. The RMU covers 3,681 acres of wild turkeys, black-walnut trees, skunks, carp, and ferns. The multipurpose 13.3-mile Reno Trail and Day Use Area are the prime outdoor recreation facilities in the unit. You have to be a tough climber because there is a 500-foot rise in elevation on the pathway. Out of breath? Okay. Pause and look at the gorgeous countryside. Hikers need to watch it in the summer as the trail also serves horseback riders. In the winter the system is groomed for snowmobiles and linked with other trails in Houston County.

A well with a hand pump is located at the parking lot—perfect placement for wiping sticky kid mouths and gummy fingers. Kids also love to pump that pump. Parents must do the obligatory "watch-me" routine.

Where: To reach the parking lot serving the trailhead, take State Highway 26 to Reno, travel west through town, and follow the meandering gravel town road for a quarter of a mile. *For more information:* Minnesota DNR Bluff Lands Coordinator, 2300 Silver Creek Road, NE, Rochester, MN 55906. Call 507-285-7432; Area Forest Supervisor, Suite 2, Agriculture Service Center, Caledonia, MN 55921. Call 507-724-5264. *Activities:* Bird-watching, fishing, hiking, hunting, picnicking, snowmobiling.

Whitewater State Park

Rain, rain, rain. Three days of drizzle can put a damper on a Memorial Day weekend. So what's there to do in a 2,700-acre park when the dog is wet, the kids are wet, and the beans are wet? Well there's no need to mope when it comes to White-water State Park. A trek in the woods and to the bluff tops can be just fine with wet-weather gear. The hike can be followed by a warm-up struggle in the Whitewater Valley visitors center lobby where a bright fire in a woodstove is always toasty on damp days. It's okay to take off your socks and warm your wet, wiggly toes.

The park, one of the state's best for year-round naturalist programs, allows guests to call wild turkeys, make maple syrup, poke around caves, watch eagles, and search for fossils. So what's a little rain when there are interpretive talks about rattle-snakes, trout fishing, and wildflower identification regularly scheduled in the visitors center auditorium. A museum and environmental exhibits in the center's Discovery Room trace the impact of humans on the Minnesota bluff lands. Best of all there are plenty of stuffed skunks, muskrats, and chipmunks on a kidsize table for hands-on experiencing. A live timber rattler even lives in the building (behind glass, of course).

For another rainy-day getaway, nearby Chimney Rock Geo-logical Center has a slide show and displays focusing on the bluff-country landscape. This center is located near the North Point picnic area, accessible off State Highway 74, which bisects the park. Chimney Rock Trail, which ascends about 1,000 feet over the valley floor from behind the facility, is a tough climb, however, wet or dry. So bring proper hiking boots and leave the wing tips at home.

Schedules of walks, evening and afternoon lectures, and demonstrations are regularly posted at the main building. Plus there are auto drives, self-guided tours, and games to play at Whitewater, making it an all-around getaway within a 90-minute drive from Rochester. Fishing for brown and rainbow trout in the Middle Branch of the Whitewater River is sometimes best in the rain, when the wily fish can't see anglers lurking along the banks or slowly wading toward their pools.

As indicated previously, most of North America was once covered by a shallow ocean. On the seabed sediment piled up and eventually became rock. At least 400 million years ago, the sea withdrew and erosion began carving out the rock formations now found in the park. Eons later Dakota Indians hunted and farmed in the vicinity, naming the river "Whitewater" because of its milky color in the spring when floods eroded the light-colored clay deposits on its banks. When white settlers moved into the region in the 1850s, they ripped off most of the original covering vegetation on the slopes. This created more erosion, which resulted in floods. Subsequently in 1919 the park was established to protect what remained of some of the natural resources in the region. The Civilian Conservation Corps built many of the existing park buildings in the 1930s, using stone quarried in the vicinity. But around the park poor soil conservation practices continued, with floods eventually forcing the abandonment of farms and some crossroads villages. Photographs in the park visitors center show this dramatic environmental downturn.

But in the 1940s the state stepped in to help local landowners with conservation measures. Planting of grass and trees and contoured farming helped immensely. Enough land was purchased to form the 2,800-acre Whitewater Wildlife Management Area adjacent to the state park. Today trails throughout the park take visitors through much of this rescued land. Two of the more difficult paths lead to the top of the ridges that overlook the park. The leg-stretching challenge, the climb, and rewarding views make them worthwhile for the serious hiker whether it rains or shines. Be sure you have strong boots with good ankle supports. The trails wind over rocks and around boulders, so there is an element of clambering and hand-holding needed. The two-and-seven-tenths-mile Coyote Point Loop of the Dakota Trail takes about two hours to traverse. The Main Loop of the Dakota Trail is four and one fifth miles, with an estimated three-and-a-half-hour-walk. But the view from the bluffs is worth the huffing and puffing. Pine, basswood, black walnut, and oaks roll away to the horizon, with occasional glimpses of the river below through the green canopy. Several of the trails (Meadow, Group Center, Beach, and Trout Run) are skiable in the winter. In 1944 and 1945 German prisoners of war were housed in a barbed-wire enclosure at the Trout Run trailhead. The POWs helped out at area farms during the war's labor shortage.

Count this next fact among the blessings at Whitewater: There are no mosquitoes! The rushing river and lack of backwater pools prevent the breeding of those generally awesome Minnesota monsters.

Where: Whitewater State Park is tucked into the bluff country of southeastern Minnesota, three miles south of the village of Elba on State Highway 74.

For more information: Whitewater State Park Manager, Route 1, Box 256, Altura, MN 55910. Call 507-932-3007.

Hours: The park is closed, except to registered campers, from 10:00 P.M. until 8:00 A.M. the following day. Loud noises are prohibited after 10:00 P.M.

Amenities: Whitewater State Park has two semimodern campgrounds with a total of 106 campsites. Four are walk-in sites, where gear must be hauled inland about 100 yards from a parking lot. There is a dump station, showers, and flush toilets. The park also features a modern group camp with cabins, dining hall, and sanitation building with showers and flush toilets, accommodating 132 persons. A primitive group camp holds 100 guests. Two picnic grounds, with a total of 150 tables, are available. There is a shelter, able to protect about 75 persons (you can pack in more folks, especially tiny tots, during a rain).

Pets: Must be leashed on restraints six feet long or less. Pets are not allowed in park buildings.

Best time to visit: Year-round (even in the rain).

Activities: Hiking, camping, fly fishing, interpretive programs, bird-watching, cross-country skiing, picnicking, museums. Motor bikes and other licensed vehicles are allowed only on designated roads.

Whitewater Wildlife Management Area

The bluff country of Minnesota is raw-stone country, with cliffs rearing above the treetops as would castles in the good old days. The Whitewater Wildlife Management Area (WWMA) includes much of the Whitewater River valley, rich in history, sights, and recreational possibilities.

The ancient fossil grounds are among the most interesting sights. A road cut shows layers of rock that date back at least 400 million years. Fossils of plants and animals that lived in the sea that once covered most of North America can be spotted in the limestone. I've never spotted a brontosaurus bone, as the fossils here even predate those giants, but there are clamlike brachiopods, sea lilies, snails, and bryozoans, which are tiny mosslike creatures.

With a bit of gumption you can see the Marnarch House, built in 1857. Nicholas Marnarch, a Luxembourg immigrant, wanted to make sure his house wouldn't blow away. It is made from locally quarried dolomitic rock and has two-and-a-half-foot thick walls. During the Sioux uprising of 1862, neighbors gathered here for protection. To reach the now-abandoned home-site, hike (or ski in the winter) about one and a half miles west on the old stagecoach road that leads to the home from the parking lot of the WWMA offices on State Highway 74. Don't go in the place, because the wear and tear of visitors may cause damage.

Weaver Bottoms is part of the Upper Mississippi River Wildlife and Fish Refuge. This is an important wetland for migrating canvasback ducks and tundra swans. Bald eagles can be spotted in abundance, their mighty wings dotting the sky as they divebomb for fish. Sometimes peregrine falcons can also be spotted by die-hard bird-watchers. The site is open for hunting during the season, with access just north of the village of Weaver.

Where: The Whitewater Wildlife Management Area is located seven miles west of State Highway 74 on Olmsted County Highway 9. The best place to park is the parking lot of an old church, about one half mile west of the cut on County Highway 9. Weaver Bottoms is at the mouth of the Whitewater River near the junction of U.S. Route 61 and County Highway 29.

For more information: Contact the John A. Latsch State Wayside Park and the Carley and Whitewater State Parks, all within or adjacent to the WWMA. Rangers at any of these sites can provide details on the management area.

Hours: The WWMA lands are open to the public from 5:00 A.M. to 10:00 P.M. daily throughout the year.

Appendix

Selected References

Charles, Craig. *Exploring Superior Country*. Minocqua,
Wisc.: Northword Press, 1992. 231 pages.

Hintz, Martin. *Country Roads of Minnesota*. Oaks, Penn.:
Country Roads Press, 1994. 159 pages. (Winner of the 1994
best travel book, Central State Chapter, Society of
American Travel Writers.)

Minnesota Department of Natural Resources. State park
trail and forest guides and public water access pamphlets.
Department of Natural Resources, Division of Parks and
Recreation.

Slade, Andrew, ed. *Guide to the Superior Hiking Trail*. Two
Harbors, Minn.: Ridgeline Press/Superior Hiking Trail
Association, 1993. 173 pages.

Umhoeffer, Jim. *Guide to Minnesota Outdoors*. Minocqua,
Wisc.: Northword Press, 1992. 279 pages.

Waters, Thomas F. *The Streams and Rivers of Minnesota*.
Minneapolis, Minn.: University of Minnesota Press, 1977.
373 pages.

Selected Agencies

Audubon Center of the North Woods
Box 530
Sandstone, MN 55072
320-245-5272 (phone and fax)

Bell Museum of Natural History
10 Church Street
Minneapolis, MN 55411
612-624-7083

Department of Natural Resources
500 Lafayette Road
St. Paul, MN 55155-4040
Information Center 651-296-6157, 888-646-6367 (toll free
from Minnesota), 800-657-3929 (TDD), 651-296-5484 (TDD)
www.dnr.state.mn.us
Division of Parks and Recreation, 651-296-9223
Division of Forestry, 651-296-4491

Hosteling International Minnesota
125 Main Southeast Street
Minneapolis, MN 55414
612-378-3773

International Wolf Center
1396 Highway 169
Ely, MN 55731
218-365-4695, 218-ELY-WOLF (218-359-9653)
or 800-475-6666

Izaak Walton League
8816 West River Road
Brooklyn Park, MN 55444
612-561-5364

Minnesota Department of Public Safety
(for biking information and registrations)
444 Cedar Street, Suite 155
St. Paul, MN 55101
651-296-6652
www.dps.state.mn.us

Minnesota Forestry Association
26 East Exchange, Suite 500
St. Paul, MN 55101
651-290-6266

Minnesota Historical Society
345 Kellogg Boulevard West
St. Paul, MN 55102-1906
651-296-6126 or 800-657-3773
www.mnhs.org.

Minnesota Native Plant Society
220 Biology Science Building
1445 Gortner Avenue
St. Paul, MN 55108
651-645-7318

Minnesota Office of Tourism
121 Seventh Place East, Suite 500
St. Paul, MN 55101-1848
651-296-5029 or 800-657-3700
(toll free from U.S. and Canada)
www.exploreminnesota.com

Sierra Club North Star Chapter
1313 Fifth Street SE, Suite 323
Minneapolis, MN 55414
612-379-3853

State Bicycle Coordinator and State Bicycle Advisory Board
MS315 Transportation Building
St. Paul, MN 55155
651-296-9966

Wildlife Forever
10365 West 70th Street
Eden Prairie, MN 55344
612-833-1522

Index

Agassiz, Louis, 5
Asbury, Bruce, 73

Beaulieu, C. H., 59
Beaver Creek Valley State Park,
    138–41
Black Dog, 105, 109
Blank, Bill, 38
Blue Mounds State Park, 117–21
Bluewater/Wabana area, 3
Bodeen, Tim, 71, 72
Bond, Ward, 86
Bronk, Leon, 156
Brower, Jacob V., 13
Buffalo at Blue Mounds State
    Park, 117–18
Buffalo River State Park, 5–6
Bunyan, Paul, 4, 74–75

Camden State Park, 121–23
Cascade River State Park, 32–35
Catlin, George, 130, 131
Central Minnesota
    activities found in, 53–55
    Charles A. Lindbergh State
        Park, 55–58
    Crow Wing State Park, 58–61
    Father Hennepin State Park,
        61–63
    Foothills State Forest/Spider
        Lake Ski Trail, 63–66
    Mille Lacs Kathio State Park
        and Rum River State
        Forest, 66–70

Moose Lake Recreational Area,
    70–71
Otter Tail County, 71–74
Paul Bunyan State Forest, 74–78
St. John's University, 78–80
Charles A. Lindbergh State Park,
    55–58
Cleveland, Ron, 108
Cloetter, Reverend Ottmar, 59
Crow Wing State Park, 58–61
Curly Head (Indian tribal leader),
    58

Dorer, Richard J., 155
Duluth, 29, 30, 48, 67, 70
Duluth, Sieur, 62, 67

Eagles, bald, 7–8, 19, 166
Eggum, Terry, 41
Elholm, John, 89

Father Hennepin State Park,
    61–63
Feikema, Elaine, 152, 153
Foothills State Forest/Spider
    Lake Ski Trail, 63–66
Forests, national
    Chippewa National Forest, 1, 3,
        6–8
    Superior National Forest, 26,
        46–49
Forests, state
    Foothills State Forest/Spider
        Lake Ski Trail, 63–66

Paul Bunyan State Forest, 74–78
Richard J. Dorer Memorial
    State Forest, 160–61
Rum River State Forest, 66–70
White Earth State Forest,
    15–19
Forestville/Mystery Cave State
    Park, 141–46
Fort Snelling State Park, 108–12

Gibbs, John, 13
Gibbs, Mary, 13
Glacial Lakes State Park, 123–25
Great River Bluffs State Park,
    154–57
Greysolon, Daniel, 67

Harris, Joel, 72
Hayes, A. F., 2
Hayes Lake State Park, 2
Heimgartner, Roger, 158
Hendel, George, 140
Hendel, Howard, 140
Hendershot, Alva, 2
Hennepin, Father Louis, 61–62,
    63, 67
Hennepin Parks
  Baker Park Reserve, 85–86
  Carver Park Reserve, 86
  Clifton E. French Regional
      Park, 88
  Crow-Hansen Park Reserve,
      86–87
  Elm Creek Park Reserve, 87
  Fish Lake Regional Park, 87–88
  general information on park
      system, 82–85
  Hyland Lake Park Reserve,
      88–90
  Murphy-Hanrehan Park
      Reserve, 90–93
Hlina, Paul, 44

Hole in the Day (Indian tribal
    leader), 58
Holland, Cliff, 10
Holmberg, Larry, 93–94, 95–96

Ingalls Wilder, Laura, 72

Jones, Casey, 160
Julson, Dina, 144

Kipp, Orrin Lansing, 154, 155
Kratoskas, Charlet and Bud, 36

La Verendrye, Pierre Goultier de,
    22, 25
Lac qui Parle State Park, 116,
    125–28
Lake Agassiz, 1, 5, 9, 114, 126
Lake Bronson State Park, 8–11
Lake Itasca State Park, 11–15
Lake Louise State Park, 147–50
Lake Shetek State Park, 128–30
Lindbergh, Charles, 55–56, 99
Lindbergh, Charles A., Sr.,
    55, 56
Lutsen-Tofte Area, 37–43
  four-wheel driving in, 41–42
  hiking trails, 39–40
  mountain biking in, 38–39
  skiing in, 37–38, 40–41
Lynd, John W., 122

Manfred, Frederick, 120
Marnarch, Nicholas, 165
McDonnell, Sue and Jack, 36
McDowell, Tom, 82–84
Meighen, Martha, 144
Meighen, Thomas, 144, 145
Metro area
  Fort Snelling State Park, 108–12
  Hennepin Parks, 82–93
  land set aside for, 81–82

Minnesota Valley National
Wildlife Refuge, 102–8
Ramsey County, 93–102
Mille Lacs Kathio State Park and
Rum River State Forest,
66–70
Minnesota, facts about, xiii. *See
also* Central Minnesota;
Metro area; Northeastern
Minnesota; Northwestern
Minnesota; Southeastern
Minnesota; Southwestern
Minnesota
Mississippi River, 11–12, 14, 58, 59,
60, 61, 68, 99, 136–38, 145, 155,
160–61
Moose Lake Recreational Area,
70–71
Morrison, Allen, 59
Mountain biking
in Lutsen-Tofte Area, 38–39
in Superior National Forest,
47–48
Moyer, Ed, 106
Murray, Elizabeth, 12
Myrick, Andrew, 115

National forests
Chippewa National Forest, 1, 3,
6–8
Superior National Forest, 26,
46–49
Nerstrand–Big Woods State Park,
151–54
Northeastern Minnesota
Boundary Waters Canoe Area
Wilderness, 30–32
Cascade River State Park,
32–35
Gunflint Trail, 35–37
Lutsen-Tofte Area, 37–43
Superior Hiking Trail, 43–46

Superior National Forest, 26,
46–49
Tettegouche State Park, 49–51
Northwestern Minnesota
Buffalo River State Park, 5–6
Chippewa National Forest, 1, 3,
6–8
Hayes Lake State Park, 2
Lake Bronson State Park, 8–11
Lake Itasca State Park, 11–15
lakes, 3–4
Red Lake River, 3
Tamarac National Wildlife
Refuge, 19–20
White Earth State Forest,
15–19
Zippel Bay State Park, 20–24

O'Brien, Tim, 20, 21, 23
Otter Tail County, 71–74
Ozawindib, 12

Parks, state
Beaver Creek Valley State Park,
138–41
Blue Mounds State Park, 117–21
Buffalo River State Park, 5–6
Camden State Park, 121–23
Cascade River State Park, 32–35
Charles A. Lindbergh State
Park, 55–58
Crow Wing State Park, 58–61
Father Hennepin State Park,
61–63
Forestville/Mystery Cave State
Park, 141–46
Fort Snelling State Park, 108–12
Glacial Lakes State Park,
123–25
Great River Bluffs State Park,
154–57
Hayes Lake State Park, 2

Lac qui Parle State Park, 116,
    125–28
Lake Bronson State Park, 8–11
Lake Itasca State Park, 11–15
Lake Louise State Park, 147–50
Lake Shetek State Park, 128–30
Mille Lacs Kathio State Park,
    66–70
Nerstrand–Big Woods State
    Park, 151–54
Rice Lake State Park, 157–60
Savanna Portage State Park, 55
Tettegouche State Park, 49–51
Whitewater State Park, 162–65
Wild River State Park, 54–55
Zippel Bay State Park, 20–24
Parson, Terry, 36
Paul Bunyan Recreational Trail, 3
Paul Bunyan State Forest, 74–78
Peake, Reverend E. Steele, 59
Pierz, Father Francis X., 59
Pike, Zebulon, 109

Ramsey, Alexander, 94
Ramsey County
    Bald Eagle Park and Otter
        Lake Regional Park, 97–98
    Battle Creek Regional Park, 97
    general information on, 93–96
    Harriet Island/Lilydale
        Regional Park, 99–100
    Hidden Falls/Crosby Regional
        Park, 100–101
    Keller-Phalen and Como
        Regional Parks, 101–2
    Lake Vadnais, 96–97
    Long Lake Regional Park, 100
    State Capitol Mall, 99
    Tamarack Nature Center, 98–99
Red Lake River, 3
Renville, Joseph, 127
Rice, H. M., 59

Rice Lake State Park, 157–60
Ryan, Tricia, 43, 45

St. Clair, Denny, 15–16
St. John's University, 78–80
Sanders, Dan, 45
Savanna Portage State Park, 55
Schoolcraft, Henry Rowe, 12
Schwarzenegger, Arnold, 153
Seglem, Dennis, 144, 145
Selness, Anne, 140, 141
Shimek, Bob, 16
Southeastern Minnesota
    Bear Lake Wetlands, 138
    Beaver Creek Valley State Park,
        138–41
    Forestville/Mystery Cave State
        Park, 141–46
    general description of, 135–38
    Great River Bluffs State Park,
        154–57
    Hay Creek Management Area,
        Richard J. Dorer
        Memorial State Forest,
        146–47
    Lake Louise State Park, 147–50
    Lamprey Pass Wildlife
        Management Area, 151
    Nerstrand–Big Woods State
        Park, 151–54
    Reno Bottoms Delta/Reno
        Management Unit,
        Richard J. Dorer
        Memorial State Forest,
        160–61
    Rice Lake State Park, 157–60
    White Wildlife Management
        Area, 165–66
    Whitewater State Park, 162–65
Southwestern Minnesota
    Blue Mounds State Park,
        117–21

Camden State Park, 121–23
Des Moines River, 116, 128
Glacial Lakes State Park,
    123–25
Lac qui Parle State Park, 116,
    125–28
Lake Shetek State Park, 128–30
Minnesota River, 113–16
Pipestone National
    Monument/Split Rock
    Creek Recreation Area,
    130–33
State Capitol Mall, 99
State facts, xiii
State forests
    Foothills State Forest/Spider
        Lake Ski Trail, 63–66
    Paul Bunyan State Forest, 74–78
    Richard J. Dorer Memorial
        State Forest, 160–61
    Rum River State Forest, 66–70
    White Earth State Forest,
        15–19
State parks
    Beaver Creek Valley State Park,
        138–41
    Blue Mounds State Park, 117–21
    Buffalo River State Park, 5–6
    Camden State Park, 121–23
    Cascade River State Park, 32–35
    Charles A. Lindbergh State
        Park, 55–58
    Crow Wing State Park, 58–61
    Father Hennepin State Park,
        61–63
    Forestville/Mystery Cave State
        Park, 141–46
    Fort Snelling State Park, 108–12
    Glacial Lakes State Park,
        123–25
    Great River Bluffs State Park,
        154–57

Hayes Lake State Park, 2
Lac qui Parle State Park, 116,
    125–28
Lake Bronson State Park, 8–11
Lake Itasca State Park, 11–15
Lake Louise State Park, 147–50
Lake Shetek State Park, 128–30
Mille Lacs Kathio State Park,
    66–70
Nerstrand–Big Woods State
    Park, 151–54
Rice Lake State Park, 157–60
Savanna Portage State Park, 55
Tettegouche State Park, 49–51
Whitewater State Park, 162–65
Wild River State Park, 54–55
Zippel Bay State Park, 20–24
Stevens, Dorothy and Darwin, 15
Strong Ground (Indian tribal
    leader), 58
Sullivan, Louis, 160
Superior Hiking Trail, 43–46
Superior National Forest, 26,
    46–49

Tettegouche State Park, 49–51
Trout Lake, 3
Tuttle, Dave and Barb, 36
Twin Cities, getaways from. *See*
    Central Minnesota
Twin Cities metro area
    Fort Snelling State Park, 108–12
    Hennepin Parks, 82–93
    land set aside for, 81–82
    Minnesota Valley National
        Wildlife Refuge, 102–8
    Ramsey County, 93–102
Two Inlets State Forest, 4

Verendrye, Pierre Goultier de la,
    22, 25
Votca, Jane, 89

Wabana Lake, 3
White, Mark, 142, 143
Whitewater State Park,
    162–65
Wild River State Park, 54–55
Wildlife refuges
    Lamprey Pass Wildlife
        Management Area, 151
    Minnesota Valley National
        Wildlife Refuge, 102–8

Tamarac National Wildlife
    Refuge, 19–20
White Wildlife Management
    Area, 165–66
Wirth, Theodore, 82

Young, Barb and Ted, 36

Zippel Bay State Park, 20–24
Zippel, William M., 22